Modern Zombies

Modern Zombies

How to Stay Ahead of the Horde and Communicate Your Way to Incredible Success

NICK LOOBY

MOLTEN PUBLISHING

Modern Zombies

How to Stay Ahead of the Horde and Communicate Your Way
to Incredible Success

First published in 2017 in Great Britain
by Molten Publishing Ltd

Molten Publishing Ltd, 14 Clachar Close,
Chelmsford, Essex, CM2 6RX

ISBN 978-0-9935929-2-8 (Paperback)
ISBN 978-0-9935929-3-5 (E-book)

www.moltenpublishing.co.uk
www.modernzombies.com

Acknowledgements

Battling the modern zombie virus takes a cool head, steely determination, and immense courage. It's a battle that can't be fought alone.

Huge thanks and appreciation to my fellow zombie slayers:

Emma and Deon at Truth.Works. who gave me the platform and the friendly guidance to discover what becoming a modern zombie slayer really feels like.

Richard and Martyn at Immersive for encouraging me to explore the adventures within these ideas.

My metaphorical-machete-wielding supporters: Louisa the Angel, Ben the Guru, and James the Inspiration.

The phenomenal talent that is Chris Kemp for taking images from my mind and making the book cover spectacular.

Lastly, my thanks go to my editor at Molten Publishing, Molly the Genius, who has been the beacon shining a light through the horde and has made sure my machete maintained its sharpness throughout.

No Armageddon can be overcome by one person. To all of you who are brave enough to face the modern zombies and show them the value of human communication, I thank you. The world needs you more now than ever before.

About the Author

Nick is a communication guy.

A speaker, a consultant, a trainer. Communication is his thing: at work, at home, and beyond.

Breathing life into organisations who are wise enough to realise they must communicate so much better. More fun, greater satisfaction, and incredible success will be their rewards when they do.

We are surrounded by an ocean of communication overwhelm, and this is giving rise to technically-blessed solutions that are removing much of what it means to be human. The zombies are here. The modern Armageddon has begun.

Nick is now a communication zombie slayer, alerting individuals, teams, and corporations to the symptoms of this most modern virus. He has the cure. There is no time to waste. You must become a zombie slayer too, and Nick will show you how.

Modern Zombies

How to Stay Ahead of the Horde and Communicate Your Way to Incredible Success

We have a serious problem with zombies.

We are infected. There is a communication virus that creeps through every home, into every office space, and can be found in every presentation hall. The world of communication is changing, becoming less human, and it will not end well.

You and I are responsible for turning this around. We can be the difference the world secretly craves. We can be the cure the world is yet to realise is indispensable. We can, and we must, defeat the rise of the *zombie* horde.

We all have a choice: join the ranks of the 'undead' and add to the noise that threatens to overwhelm us all, or rise up, wield our metaphorical machetes, and become communication zombie slayers.

In theory, it has never been easier to be heard by your audience. My smartphone alone has more than thirty apps that enable me, in one form or another, to communicate with my fellow human. We have never been more *connected* as we are today. We do, however, lack real human *connection*. The truth is, it has never been more difficult to truly get through to those you wish to interact with.

Our communication has become anaemic; it lacks the power to impact in a way that serves us. There's plenty of it, but like doing your dishes in the bath, there is more waste than effect. Our digital realm has made things simple, but that does not mean communicating well is easy.

Look around you. Pause for a moment and let the scene soak in. What do you see? What do you really see? I guarantee you are surrounded by a world playing it safe. Streams of people have one eye on their technology, never stepping off the map where true adventure begins.

What we see everywhere are screens: glorious, beautiful, highly defined screens. They look so good. Their colours are sharper than the real world. They entice us to come closer as they share their hypnotising clarity. We are drawn in, hungry; like a mirage in the desert, they promise salvation, and we are not disappointed — they have everything we could ever need. We love them and cannot be separated.

We are surrounded by a younger, seemingly comfortable generation worshipping these screens. They share their secrets, feed on the world's knowledge, and live their lives *through* this technological heaven rather than *around* it. A vast number of the population opt to observe the world through filters rather than seeing it for how it truly is. They are living their lives through the adventures of others. The first question on the lips of this generation relates to connectivity — if the Wi-Fi is not up to standard, they're having a nightmare.

You inhabit offices filled with grey. Fingers dancing on keyboards in a constant rhythm, nourishing the ever-hungry monitors, drowning in email. I see presenters hiding behind their displays, sharing dated knowledge, repurposing tired material, lazy in their approach, their audiences more interested in their own portable universes.

We have *friends* sharing their lives from machine to machine, constantly updating and feeding layer upon layer of content into a world already bursting with noise. These invasions of our crowded space are unwanted, uninvited, and unwelcome.

I see *progress,* and I wonder where our adventures have gone? Where is the person who dares to stand tall and share their authentic voice, who has the courage to show their passion and communicate with power and heartfelt purpose in a human way?

We are evolving and leaning towards the *safety* of technology, and somewhere along the line, we are losing part of who we really are. We are, on the one hand, liberated, but we do not appreciate the cost of our freedom.

We live in a time of Armageddon. A communication virus is turning us into modern zombies, and we are losing chunks of our humanness.

It's difficult to remember a time before our screens ruled our lives. There is no going back, only forwards to a world of more. Faster, brighter, slimmer, more connected, easier to access. Everything we need, and a host of things we don't yet know we need, delivered instantly, effortlessly, constantly.

We have come so far, so rapidly. Our progress is incredible.

Deloitte's mobile consumer survey from 2016 suggests that 81% of all UK adults and 91% of 18-44-year-olds owns a smartphone.[1] These figures continue to grow and don't include the other devices that allow us to communicate one-to-one or one-to-many.

More concerning than the incredible rise of the machine is the fact that 34% of us check our phones in the middle of

---

1   Deloitte LLP consumer survey, 2016

the night, 68% use their smartphone while having dinner with their family, and 81% are on their devices while watching TV.

The world of analogue communication has passed. We are now digital, and we love it.

The communication virus is pulling us away from our truly human interactions. There is barely any room and time to develop rapport, to experience true empathy, and to connect on a human level. Communication is fast becoming the realm of the *zombie,* and we are losing sight of the land of the *real.*

On my most recent birthday, I received approximately a hundred Facebook notifications, fourteen cards, and five phone calls. Only fourteen cards on my birthday! But hold on, Nick. Don't panic. You received a hundred greetings on Facebook. This prevailing practice reflects how communication has evolved, and we have all seen it. It is cheaper, easier, and more convenient to communicate in a digital way than the old-fashioned, time-consuming methods of the past. Herein lies an unspoken problem, a problem that is giving rise to the modern zombie. With ease and expediency, we lose much of the human sentiment of previous communication. If we're not careful, we bring our communication to the level of a transactional exchange.

Human-to-human communication has become an art practised by the minority. When and how did that happen? When did we let that happen? We are so reliant on our technology to aid our communication journey that we no longer have to, or want to, meet face to face. Our conversations have a battle simply to be heard, and our language is evolving into a short, emoji-filled ticker tape.

I'm not proposing we unplug our machines, light candles, and congregate around the campfire. I am suggesting we fight the virus and slay the communication zombies by stepping off the map and slowing down to interact in a way that has a genuine impact on our fellow humans.

Great communication gets through and makes a difference. Things actually happen rather than the perception that things have occurred. People listen, understand, are moved to action, growth, and change. Greater satisfaction and achievement are our rewards. More success, fulfilment, and fun can be ours, but we have a battle on our hands.

Who knew it would be a battle? All these amazing advancements in communication technology are, on the one hand, a massive ally, but on the other, a huge hindrance to the human resonance that it takes to truly get through to our audience.

I am suggesting a fresh approach to communication. It is radical because it relies on human-to-human interaction. This used to be the norm, but now it is an art. It is easier to send an email, to post a tweet, and to update your Facebook status, but it is nowhere near as powerful as human communication delivered by individuals that care. We can and we must choose to be the modern *zombie slayers* and battle this rampant communication virus.

If you have the heart to get through, the hunger to deliver messages that stick, and the desire to have conversations that move your audience to greater success, then pick up your metaphorical machete. Together we can, and must, change the world.

SECTION 1

Sensing the Zombie and Communicating with Yourself

"Until you step into the unknown, you
don't know what you're made of."
— Roy T. Bennett

To battle against the communication virus, you will need to have courage, an eye for real adventure, and be ready to undertake a phenomenal journey.

I am concerned that imagination is being sucked from us, replaced by a smorgasbord of apps that feed us ideas, activity, and action. If we can focus and concentrate long enough, we may be verging on a digital adventure, but don't hold your breath.

During childhood, imagination is an incredible companion and forms our view of how adventures can transpire. If we think back, we can all remember a time when our imagination provided a large proportion of our *adventures*. Before we reached the age of independence, our hands were tied, and we had to make the most of the opportunities we had and the tools at our disposal. Fortunately, our creativity knew no bounds.

As a thoughtful child, for a time, even a jar of buttons was enough to while away hours of 'alone' time for me. I remember a two-week period of illness where I was safely confined to my Grandmother's house. No idea what she had done to deserve the dubious pleasure of looking after a sick child, but there I was, confined to safety and boredom with mostly my imagination as company.

For two weeks, I remained hidden, and I populated my world with a jar of buttons.

Not the most exciting of playthings, I admit, but add a dose of imagination and a bundle of resourcefulness, and you have everything you need for *adventures*. Within the jar, there were your everyday, standard shirt buttons and occasional grander jacket buttons. Some of the more enigmatic buttons held a particular attraction. They were individuals with mysterious histories, and I couldn't picture them attached to any one piece of clothing. These were my stars and took a leading role in most of my fireside voyages.

After each *adventure,* the buttons would slide back into the jar, sealed with a twist and a click and sit patiently, awaiting a future moment of wonder.

You may have many fond memories of simpler times where 'make-believe' was a full-time occupation. No doubt one of the reasons the *Toy Story* movies resonated with such a large audience was our pre-teen ability to enable most of our toys to possess a 'voice' as we shared their adventures.

For most of us, the explorations of our younger years are replaced by responsibility and adult obligations, but our sense of adventure should grow as our opportunities and freedom develop.

One of the healthiest attitudes to carry and use in your communication battle is to embrace all of your adventures, large and small. Real adventures are not found in a jar of buttons but can be discovered around every corner if we dare to open our eyes, allow ourselves a moment to think creatively, and let our imaginations free to work their magic.

The modern 'jar of buttons' are readily available on every device. They suck us in and dissolve our time and feed the virus that leads to the modern zombie.

Allow me to share one of the biggest secrets of our time.

The adventures are everywhere.

They are longing to be embraced and made your own. The digital world has grown expert at hiding them from us.

Stop for a moment and consider the last time you had a real adventure: at work, at home, or beyond. What risks did you take? How far out of your comfort zone were you? Could you feel the adrenaline course through your veins as you stepped into the unknown?

Really stop and think.

What do you reckon?

Does something spring to mind accompanied by a cheeky grin and a feeling of being alive, or are you struggling to recount anything out of the ordinary?

Why do I suggest that the idea of 'adventures everywhere' is some kind of secret? As children, this was no secret. It was more like our code of conduct as we explored the new, the untried, and the mountainous uncertainty of youth.

There has been a shift, and our explorations have been replaced by search engines. There is no trial and error any more. There is YouTube, the solution in easy steps, tried, tested, and peer-reviewed. Any answer we seek is available, instantly, in multiple formats across any device. A utopia of free information supports our every move.

In many ways, this is phenomenal. How useful is it to have the answer on hand, almost always? But there is a casualty of this technology nirvana, and that is the spirit of adventure. The discovery of 'new ways' to complete a task, innovations from trial and error, and mistakes that reveal hidden gems.

I noticed this, firstly, with my children, who never knew a time before search engines. They've always had access to the world's knowledge and quick fixes to almost every problem or enquiry. Their world was populated by amazing technology, developing and improving almost too quickly to see. For them, there was no need to run through the woods with make-believe guns fashioned out of sticks, sharing their version of machine gun noises with friend and foe alike. Why would they when they could switch on their game console, plug in their headphones, and disappear into an immersive battlefield of technical brilliance and play 'life-like' games with a global team?

Technology, with all its far-reaching and enabling majesty, is turning the dial down on our sense of adventure. Our experiences are muted, many of them virtual, lived through the eyes of others who are kindly sharing their magic online. It's awesome, but it isn't ours.

Think again and consider your most recent adventure. It doesn't have to be big, doesn't require sharing on social media, no need for it to go viral; it's you, doing your thing, in your way. Quirky, brilliant, amazing you and your stuff. What does it look like, how does it sound, and how does it feel? Does it make you smile, fill you with pride and an air of satisfaction?

It should. It must.

We owe it to ourselves, to our teams, our audience, to have adventures that stir the emotions and make us buzz with all that is human. This is our cure and must be shared.

Most of the world's greatest thinkers, business owners, and thought leaders have stories of adventure: how they have overcome the unfamiliar, the challenging, and the downright impossible.

Take a moment to look ahead and wonder where your journey will take you. What is around this next corner? What doors will this task open? What outcomes await from this challenge? What magic lays in wait if I, and my team, attempt this?

The greatest leaders of the future will be explorers, and they will inspire their tribes to have amazing adventures.

I'm going to suggest something rather strange. Put this book down, for now, and seek out an adventure. We rarely give ourselves the time to stop and consider the majesty of the amazing world we inhabit, let alone explore the unknown.

For those of you on a lunch break or stealing some time between meetings, here is an opportunity to stretch yourself, physically and emotionally. Put the book down for five minutes, stand, look around, and head in a new direction. Walk somewhere you have not been for a while. Another department, team space, or even outside the office. Stand tall and proud and observe. Someone not too far away is about to be complimented. Be brave. Say hello to the next person who passes by, compliment them on their clothing, hair, shoes, office, the way they carry themselves, or anything that catches your eye. Bask in the magic of a human interaction. Strike up a conversation if the moment allows. Introduce yourself and interact.

If you are commuting, close the book and look around. Someone nearby is going to join you on this adventure. Strike up a conversation. Tell them Nick said to say hi and ask how their day is going.

If you're sitting quietly in a coffee shop, then similarly, look up and observe. There is a conversation awaiting your courageous introduction. Hi, I'm reading this book, and Nick has suggested I have a human conversation, do you have five minutes?

If you are at home, congratulations. Put the book to one side and give yourself five minutes. Pick up your phone and ring your brother, sister, mum, dad, best friend, or someone randomly selected from your address book. Say hi and let them know you were thinking of them. No need to go into a lengthy conversation, unless that works for you, but most definitely say hi.

Every day we spend, on average, 8 hours and 41 minutes on our media devices.[2]

2   Ofcom Communications Market Report, 2017

This amount of time feeds your zombie but not your adventures. Time for a change.

You have, no doubt, witnessed the communication *infection* sucking the fun and adventure from your daily interactions. Even those personalities who could be relied upon to innovate, enthuse, and inspire are becoming shells of their previous colourful selves. Far too easily we are sliding towards a grey shadow of communication that is neither practical nor invigorating.

I wonder how many of you actually put the book down and interacted? How many adventures took place? How many of you texted a loved one rather than called them?

Our goal must be to rid the world of the rapidly spreading communication virus. To lead the charge of the new communicators who revel in the human to human. Even if we are online, you will sense the human, right there, breathing life into the technology.

Imagine if your next email began as follows:

Hi Dave,

Before I ask some questions about 'x' project, I just want to check in and see how you're doing. How are the family? What are your highlights from the year so far?

Can you imagine the look on Dave's face?

I am concerned that this kind of email introduction is most likely considered ridiculous. We are too busy to faff around asking personal questions. It's not appropriate in a work environment. It's not considered professional. We run the risk of a call from HR to discuss our behaviour. This is the world we have created. Why do we fear the human? Dare we even raise the machete?

Surely we want to have more escapades, find more satisfaction at work and beyond, and become successful through powerful communication? We, the zombie slayers, are coming. We are outnumbered, and our journey will take considerable courage, but we are here, and we will be heard.

Self-Talk

"A man cannot directly choose his
circumstances, but he can choose his
thoughts, and so indirectly, yet surely,
shape his circumstances."
— James Allen

A number of years ago, I faced a challenge which I have managed to reframe as an amazing adventure. At the time, I didn't know the experience was going to teach me some of life's most valuable lessons. It was, on the one hand, incredibly serious, and on the other, strangely comical.

I went for lunch with my boss, a cosy, local Italian with subdued lighting and flavour-rich scents lingering in the air. It was a place she regularly used but a bit of a treat for me, and my mouth watered at the anticipation of some succulent pasta and perhaps even a glass of something deep and crimson.

During the chatty and relaxed meal, my boss asked me what turned out to be a very loaded question:

"What would you really like to do, Nick?"

What a lovely question, I thought. This conversation is about to get philosophical. Here's an opportunity to open up and share. I regularly asked this question of my training course delegates during icebreaker introductions.

I straightened up in my chair. This was a question I was more than ready to answer. My response was brief, honest, told with excitement, and in the spirit of the conversation as it developed.

"Geraldine, I would love to run my own training company."

In retrospect, this was a foolish answer in a conversation that turned out to have life-changing repercussions. It's one of those conversations you replay in your head to see if there was an intonation you missed or a signal that was loud and clear that passed straight over your head.

My body language and people-reading skills are so much better these days, but if there was something I should have seen during that conversation, I didn't spot it, and I talked openly and freely.

That was a mistake.

A week later, I was in the boss's office, and she broke the news that she was making me redundant! A job that I had been doing for three years and desperately needed to keep — gone. An hour after that, I was leaving the office for the last time with a cardboard box filled with my belongings.

It sounds (and looked) like something straight out of a Hollywood script. All I needed was a backing track playing some depressing music and the heavens to open as soon as I stepped onto the street, and the scene would be ready for the cinema.

Bugger.

I was numb. I really didn't see it coming. Grim thoughts crashed through my mind. I saw nothing but trouble ahead. The temporary fog of doom began to cloud my vision.

A surprise redundancy is rarely welcome, and this one came at a really difficult time for me personally. The timing couldn't have been much worse. But, as with every event that occurs in your world, you can choose how to respond, how you deal with the outcome and the fallout.

Do you roll over, hide, moan at the injustice of the world (become a bit zombie), and lick your wounds, or do you respond with courage, with determination, and with fire in your belly?

It's up to you. You get to choose.

"Between stimulus and response there is a space. In that space is our power to choose our response."
— Viktor Frankl

Once the haze of anxiety lifted, I chose my response.

First thing the next day, I was on the phone discussing options with my favourite clients. The training company, that really was a deep-seated ambition of mine, was born! I spoke to a huge number of people and asked them if they would buy from my brand-new company, and I was blown away by the response. For most of my clients, their driver was that they had a relationship with me, and this surpassed the connection they had with my old company.

My dream of running my own company, helping others to maximise their success by communicating with real passion and power, had begun.

I formed my training company and set out on the challenging but fulfilling journey that continues to this day, and I'm loving every minute of it. Well, not every minute. It is a business after all, and business is tough. I'm following my dream; does it get more exciting than that? All of you who are currently pursuing your vision know how this feeling bubbles inside and drives you forward with incredible energy. You need this energy though; business is hard work, and there are countless steps in numerous directions before you realise the progress you are making. I had so much to learn, still do in fact, but what a ride!

Sometimes life will present you with opportunities that initially look like setbacks. Indeed, most setbacks can be turned around. They are temporary hurdles that can launch you into something truly life-changing. It's up to you how you look at these 'hurdles', these challenges, these opportunities, and how you turn them into the adventures that will define who you are and how successful you will become.

> "Accept reality, but focus on the solution. Take that issue, take that setback, take that problem, and turn it into something good. Go forward. And, if you are part of a team, that attitude will spread throughout." — Jocko Willink[3]

I learnt a great deal about myself during this redundancy episode. I learnt that ambition, if big enough, will drive you and make the moving of mountains a possibility. I also learnt a huge amount about the people I held most dear, who cared about my future and my wellbeing.

People can be magical, and given the right conditions, they will be right behind you, providing some of the energy that is essential to carry you through to a successful outcome. Zombies aren't magical.

The first substantial stepping stone which provides the basis for healthy communication 'attitudes' is to cultivate an amazing relationship with yourself and to communicate in a constructive way with *you*. Choose your responses. Take

---

3   From *Tools of Titans* by Tim Ferriss, 2016 – Jocko Willink talking about 'Extreme Ownership'

ownership and be your own biggest fan. We're losing this ability in the modern zombie Armageddon. Too often our digital devices surround us with critical thinking, negative outlooks, unachievable standards, and things that simply aren't real.

I'm not suggesting we all begin to talk to ourselves out loud (although I do enjoy this, and not just because of the looks on the faces of those around me), but I am most definitely suggesting we start to make changes that create a healthier self-perception. This will provide our basic defence against the oncoming virus.

Let's explore your attitude for a moment.

Imagine a hurdle that you face right now. Consider how it makes you feel and how you are going to overcome it. Give it some thought, we have time. Any hurdle, doesn't have to be huge, but it can be if you wish. It's all yours.

You have a room to decorate, a project to plan, a presentation to prepare, an important meeting to attend, a difficult conversation to have, a painful choice to make, a lengthy journey to embark upon, a traffic jam to endure, a bridge to build, or a hole to dig.

Now change the language you use regarding this 'hurdle' and simply refer to it, in your mind and out loud, as a 'challenge'. Simply changing our language will affect how we communicate with ourselves and how we see the task ahead. We are fighting the virus while those around us are succumbing to the infection.

How does it feel as a challenge as opposed to a hurdle? A hurdle is something to be overcome, a blockage, and we have to find a way over or our path will be limited. A challenge is something to get us thinking, something to be outwitted, and something that will cause us to raise our game; to overcome a challenge makes us better, stronger, and more resilient.

Now take this a step further. Consider this challenge, reframe it in your mind, and replace the word 'challenge' with the word 'adventure'. Embrace the task at hand as an adventure rather than a challenge. Think about the 'adventure' that lies ahead. Adventures are where excitement and the unknown reside. They are recounted to us as stories over dinner and related down the pub with our mates. Feel the excitement of experiencing this adventure and living to tell the tale.

Let's look at an example.

I have an opportunity. I am speaking at an event filled with members of the military. The event is designed to be a combination of networking and recruitment discussions for those in the process of leaving the armed forces. Many of the audience has already left the military and are there to share their experiences of what a civilian work environment has in store and how it compares to the one they left behind.

The *hurdles* I face:

1. I want them to see the essential value of emotional communication in the civilian world.
2. Military interactions are typically disciplined and efficient with little room for anything emotional.
3. I haven't served in the military.

Time for a reframe.

The *challenges* I have:

1. Communicating in a way that resonates and gets through so I can affect change and save some marriag-

es, careers, and perhaps a few lives along the way.

2. Build rapport and empathise from the perspective of my military knowledge (I was raised in a military household and attended a military school).

A further step.

The *adventures*:

1. I can be emotional, sharing from the heart, based on the mistakes I have made, and I can bring my story to life with humour — it's going to be fun!
2. At last, some magic to be taken from a shitty boarding school upbringing.

Prepare your communication with the adventures in mind, and your audience will thank you for it.

I delivered my talk.

It was amazing. I shared some personal stuff and some tough lessons learned. I used humour to highlight what was at stake and how my lack of emotional communication in the past had seriously held me back. My audience loved it. They were entertained, and the hugely important messages stuck. It was delivered in the style of a conversation: no slides, no notes, no room for a glimmer of communication virus. In a zombie-laden world, my message got through.

From here on in, I am going to ask you to do things differently again and again, as this is where the fun is, where change occurs and will have the greatest impact on your future.

Your New Orbit

The more you stretch that comfort zone of yours, the more you will dare to believe, and amazing things will begin to occur once you take action.

In fact, the idea of stepping out of your *comfort zone* doesn't do this justice. I've heard the phrase too often, and it's become stale. Zombies love these anaemic phrases because they take minimal effort and mean you don't have to communicate with creativity and thought. Wherever you hear the following phrases beware, zombies lurk:

- *thinking outside the box*
- *at the end of the day*
- *give you a heads-up*
- *take that offline*
- *we must move the needle*
- *we're experiencing negative growth*
- *do you have the bandwidth?*
- *we must leverage synergies*
- *run it up the flagpole* (this one makes me cringe the most)

What I'm asking you to do is to step into a new *orbit*. Your new orbit represents everything you strive to be and is far removed from all that is cosy in your comfortable bubble.

Zombies love the bubble. They shuffle round and round under the misconception of safety in numbers.

The creation and delivery of the *Invisible PowerPoint* show was a new *orbit* for both me and for my audience. The *Invisible PowerPoint* show has taken me all around the country and has been delivered to diverse audiences. It only takes an hour and changes the way we communicate with groups forever. The book (of the same name) was a massive learning curve. The journey was dramatic and asked some tough questions of how I and my audience were choosing to communicate.

Speaking on stage with an audience of hundreds used to be a comfort zone thing, and auditioning and appearing on the TEDx platform was a new *orbit*. The steps are bigger, bolder, and the rewards so much greater than the old *zone*. It's the place to be, stretching yourself again and again to become the most amazing version of you imaginable.

Consider your current *normal*. Think about your daily adventures and where they sit within this zone. How often do you stretch yourself, dare to fail, take risks and live life on the *dark side*? When was the last time you volunteered to attempt something new at work or outside the office?

When did you last stand tall and offer to present to your team? When did you last agree to fill in for the missing chair of your monthly meeting? How long has it been since you took on some additional duties that are not your core strength? How tempted are you to write the questions for the weekly pub quiz night? When did you last join a community group to challenge some local injustice? Can you remember the last time you turned off the TV and took steps to learn a new hobby?

In your new *orbit,* all of these things can be yours. Forget *comfort zones*, we have moved beyond them — we are in our new world, and the amazing modifications begin here.

It's not a question of *bandwidth*; it is a choice. Take a moment and choose something. Right now. Something a little outrageous, stretching, out of reach. Something that makes you smile, makes you nervous, something that may raise a few eyebrows. Say it, write it down, post it on a note, pin it to your wall, or stick it on your PC. Make it visible. Don't allow yourself to hide from it. Embrace it. Tell your friends, and take a step in the new direction. Give yourself a timeframe for the first step and stick to it.

Be the change that will determine who you will become. Begin. The journey awaits.

Congratulations, you have begun. Sounds too good to be true, but it's not. It can be yours. You just have to stick with it, be prepared to get your hands dirty, and work at it. It may be simple, but this doesn't mean it is easy.

If your orbit looks and feels zombie, it's time for change.

Does this sound like you? Are you part of the horde? You wake, still tired, exhausted even. You drag yourself from the warmth and comfort of your duvet and haul yourself into another day. Squeezed between sleepers and screen-locked mutes, you bump along your commute to work. Nothing about today looks different from yesterday, and tomorrow already looks frighteningly similar. Trudging towards the office, passing countless versions of yourself, growls rising from crowds, you find yourself snarling your displeasure as it's echoed from every part of the zombie mass.

Another day, then another and another await...

Will your journey look any different? Will you take strides to carve out an alternative to now? Is your hunger more than that of the zombie horde? Do you have the appetite for positive change, to develop a calling and throw everything you have at it?

I would be more than happy to share the journey into your new orbit and catalogue the steps to a successful outcome. Feel free to contact me at nick@feetontheground. co.uk, and I will do my best to share your story with the world — that should provide a healthy dose of motivation for you.

If you like a challenge, then you are in good company. I love a challenge. It feeds the hunger inside that strives for success, even if that success is based on a task I set myself. Often, we need to enter a new orbit to achieve these ambitions — we have to become a different person. A new us turns up and takes on the new.

You've really got to want it, so set yourself goals that have real meaning to you and keep track of your progress. Become the success you crave.

Self-Belief

"With realization of one's own potential
and self-confidence in one's ability, one
can build a better world." — Dalai Lama

Many years ago, I ran a training course on some technology I was only just beginning to master. I was in one of those catch-22 situations. I was still learning how this stuff worked, but my client wanted the benefit of my expertise *now*. The question on my mind was, 'when will I really be ready to train others?', but the question on my client's mind was, 'can you come in this week?'.

In the early days of working for myself, it was very difficult to say no to work, so I said, *"Yes, this week will be fine."* Hmmm, interesting choice, Nick.

We were all about to learn how well I really knew this technology.

As it turned out, I knew it *reasonably* well. Reasonably is not what most client's desire though. I did OK, but I was floundering at certain points during the course, especially when the tech began to behave erratically (doesn't it always?). My clients were lovely though. They forgave my uncertainty, and the course was a partial success. Did I tell you I'm not a perfectionist? Not even close as it turns out. I was lucky with this particular client; I have met many more demanding ones since.

I have continued to train on this particular piece of communication technology, and over a decade later, I have wrestled with every imaginable scenario and have worked with hundreds of world-class companies. I am now the go-to expert in many parts of the UK, but it had to start somewhere. Often, it starts in a place that is rather daunting. Not as terrifying as a horde of zombies, hungry for brains, beating a path to your door, but pretty scary.

That first step was the most nerve-racking and the most difficult — like most first times, they are not the best performance you are likely to witness, but they are a must if you are going to develop into a professional.

If you can communicate your ideas, your enthusiasm, and your desire to see the world from your client's perspective and help them to improve, then almost any task can be yours to command.

Consider what you have to offer that is totally yours, a unique take on your area of expertise, your version of magic, ideas, and stories that belong to you and you alone. How can you package and deliver this so audiences remember you and easily recall how you helped them see clearer than they have ever seen before? It's going to take courage and steely determination, but that's you. This is what being a zombie slayer looks and feels like. You can separate yourself from the horde and show the world what you are made of.

Each of us is unique. We have some incredible gifts to share, but we tend to hide behind our technology — welcome to Zombieland. Too readily we ease onto the road most travelled rather than taking a risk and stepping into a stranger orbit where amazing change can occur.

Commit and take the first step towards your dream, ambition, or transformation. Have the nerve, the audacity even, to share your story in a unique way. You won't find a zombie with this much courage.

I find that any challenge raises an initial question, and that is, 'do I believe I can do this?' If the task is simple and your response is, "of course, no problem", you may not have set the bar high enough.

If you always achieve all of the goals you set yourself, it's worth checking you don't have your sights too low; it's worth taking a bigger risk, often. A moment of internal questioning is a healthy thing.

Think of your new orbit. If you previously wrote something down and pinned it on your wall or PC, firstly, thank you, and secondly, how likely is your success?

Give yourself a score between 1 and 10: 1 being *I don't have a hope in hell* (set yourself a different orbit challenge if this is the case), and 10, *I am totally convinced I will succeed* (make sure it is enough of a challenge before you embark on your adventure).

If you are around the 7 mark (or below), I would be worried. Is your heart really in this? Are you hungry enough? What's stopping you from making it a 10?

If you put your score at 8 or 9, I am still worried for you, maybe even more so. Make sure you haven't given yourself a score that leaves room for a few well-timed, comfortable excuses. You are so close to that magical 10.

How many zombies do you know that have 10 on 10 challenges ahead?

Of course, we live in the real world, and all of our challenges will not end in success and jubilation. Life is not that easy or predictable. If I pick up an injury, I may not be able to complete a running challenge I have set myself, for example. But if the outcome is within your control, outside a case of rotten luck or unforeseen misfortune, do you believe, wholeheartedly, you will succeed? If so, where is your 10?

I know many people who set themselves a challenge: to give up smoking, to get out of debt, to go a month without drinking. But they are not 10 out of 10 committed. Their scores lack the true self-belief that makes the difference between success and failure.

I often ask audiences if they have set themselves a recent challenge or New Year's resolution to test some of the zombie traits. It's rare to find many who have fulfilled their ambition and completed their challenges to their satisfaction.

If the goal we have set (if you haven't set one yet, I'll happily set one for you[4]) doesn't excite us enough to believe totally in our success, then we need to have a word with ourselves.

"What are you playing at? Set a decent goal. Don't hide behind the easy stuff. Engage with the hard-core challenge that will transform your world — yesssss, that's the stuff. Bring it on!"

If everything in life were easy, I'm not sure if it would be blissful or boring. For me, the things I most desire require real focus, clarity, and grit. But they will be mine. As long as I don't have Bond-villain-style expectations, all will be well.

---

4   For those of you who have not made a commitment to a goal, I suggest the following: commit to a random act of kindness today and make it happen. Once complete, you can focus on a goal of your own. Excellent work.

Too many people don't believe they are in control of their own destiny; they don't feel in the driving seat of their lives. For these people, and they are everywhere, life just happens to them. They are victims of circumstance rather than the *creators* of circumstance.

> *"I can't alter my future. I am simply dealing*
> *with the cards I have been given."*

A typical victim of circumstance (zombie) viewpoint. If you know anything about cards, especially poker, then you will know that the person with the best cards doesn't always win. You can be outplayed by someone with nothing. I once outplayed an entire table of Vegas poker players with a pair of twos. It's rarely about what you have been dealt.

Don't settle for 'the cards' you currently have. Make some healthy choices and select a different hand. Become a creator of circumstance and decide what you want your future to look like, and then make the choices that will take you there.

I'm not suggesting it will be easy (it may be, but usually it isn't). To grip the steering wheel of your life's direction is both empowering and essential if we are to deliver the success we deserve. Empowering choices are not the realm of the zombie.

Believe in your power to stay the course, take the wheel, and steer towards your destination. Don't forget to keep your vehicle (you) topped up with fuel and well serviced — in other words, treat your body and your mind well. Stay fit, eat healthy, and sleep plenty. Oh, and enjoy the journey.

Against the Odds

A client of mine, a local politician, is a prime example of what self-belief can deliver. Determined to change the standing of his party in the local area, his conviction and energy were his greatest assets, and we worked on his communication skills to enable him to spread the word more effectively.

If he didn't believe it was possible to change the view of the population (or a large proportion of it), we stood zero chance of making it a reality.

It was a tough job. The area historically held opposing views, and the likelihood of ultimate success (election) was slim. But even when the odds are against us, should we cease to believe? At what point should we be 'realistic' and temper our beliefs? At what point does optimism become unhealthy?

A difficult question to answer, but we all know of those who have succeeded against the odds, and we also know those who have not quite made it.

With a tremendous amount of work put into his campaign, my client increased the margin for his party more than any other in the county, and in doing so, bucked the national trend. Did he win? Not officially and not according to the voting population. Was he right to believe? Most definitely.

With belief comes commitment, with commitment comes action, and with action we create our futures.

If we truly believe, our behaviours change, and once our behaviours are on track, positive results will follow.

If the voice inside the toilets on a Virgin train suggests you should not flush your 'hopes and dreams', who are we to disagree? They really do. It's quirky but true. They also suggest you don't flush goldfish or your ex-girlfriend's jumper. Lovely communication, thank you, Virgin.

Ultimately, it comes down to the choices we make. Notice I did not say the choices of others. These are *ours*, and therein lies the real power. Our online world is filled to bursting with the choices of others. We are drowning in the opinions and viewpoints of others, and our voice is lost in this ocean of noise. Our real zombie-slaying power comes from our individuality, our choices, and our unique take on all subjects to be communicated.

Whatever our lives look like, whatever occurs, we get to choose how we respond to the situation we find ourselves in. We may not have created the environment or circumstance, but we can definitely decide how we react.

Consider for a moment an event that you have experienced recently and think about how you responded to that experience. Take your time. I imagine most of you will arrive at a troublesome incident, and thinking about it, you may have reacted less than favourably. Someone cut in front of you in the car and you exchanged some heated gesticulations perhaps, or you're delayed on your journey to work, and you curse the gods for making your life a misery!

A little while ago, I had a busy day planned in London and bought a travel card that allows unlimited travel on London's tube and bus service. It's a single ticket that you use in all the machines to access and exit the tube. Upon approaching my first (of many) ticket machines of the day, my ticket was not accepted. Hmm. I tried again, and no joy. OK, probably an issue at that particular gate, so no problem. I found a guard, and they let me through a gate manually. On arrival at my destination, the exit gate didn't play ball either — bugger. It seemed as though my ticket was a dud, so I had to find a member of staff to let me out of the station.

At this point, I had some choices to make. I could get annoyed, curse my luck, abuse the technology which is not working as it should, or worse, abuse the staff who, by association, are surely to blame. Or I can choose a more positive and more satisfying response. I could have had the ticket replaced with one that functioned correctly, but I decided to let it roll and reserved myself to having conversations with staff members at every entrance and exit throughout my journey for the day.

I am a communication guy after all. I simply turned what, to most, would be a bit of a pain, into an opportunity to converse with several strangers, and I looked forward to those brief conversations throughout the day. I actually enjoyed the fact that my ticket was 'defective'.

That's what it comes down to — choices. How you choose to respond *is totally up to you.*

Now, consider your event again, and think about an alternative choice you could have made. Could you forgive the fool who cut you up in the car, even feel sorry for them? After all, they're living their life at a speed that can only be stress-ridden. Could you treat your delay into work as an opportunity to make a phone call to someone you haven't spoken to in an age or as bonus time to read, converse, or play a game of lookie-likey?

For those of you unfamiliar with 'lookie-likey', it's a simple observation game. Look around and spot all the people who look, in any way, like someone famous. It works best if you share your observations with a friend. It's unlikely they will agree, but that's part of the fun. Discretion is your ally in this game. Enjoy.

It takes a bit of getting used to, allowing yourself to choose a better way, a healthier choice, an option that is more fun, more productive, and actually adds value to your world. But it is up to you. You have the power to make that choice, and it will determine the universe you exist in and how fulfilling your orbit will become.

Invisible Coach

"You are today where your thoughts
have brought you; you will be tomorrow
where your thoughts take you."
— James Allen

One of the ways I make choices that serve me well and make my life such an adventure is through a healthy relationship with my invisible coach. My coach lives inside my head, and you have one in there too.

What's going on inside that truly amazing brain of yours is a mass of information processing, filtering, sorting, and storing. It's happening all the time, and it's incredible. We're kind of magic that way.

The brain is busy. It's all going on, and it's a mass of traffic in there. So much information is being processed, that the brain has to filter out the stuff we don't need; otherwise, we may explode. (OK, that might be taking it a bit far, but we certainly won't be operating with any useful clarity.)

There are things going on that you don't need to know about and you are unaware of until it is mentioned and therefore focused on. If I ask you to focus on what your tongue feels like in your mouth, does it feel as though your mouth is full? Focus on your tongue, and suddenly it becomes alive and probably begins to check out the backs of your teeth. Until I asked though, you probably hadn't given it a second thought.

What's happening here is your amazing 'noggin' filtering out the stuff that's not worth thinking about until, for whatever reason, it becomes the focus of attention. Usually our brain is on our side and is phenomenal at filtering and finding the information we need, whenever we need it.

There are exceptions, of course, such as trying to remember the name of that person who you have just seen approaching, who you met at that event a month ago and for the life of you can't place. Nope. It's gone. It's on the tip of your tongue, but can you recall it in time? No. Typical.

Your invisible coach is there to work with the most useful parts of your brain and find all the positive things: the memories, references, and examples that we need to bolster our efforts and give us the encouragement required to tackle a task with optimism.

Danger, danger! The invisible coach is not alone. You also have an invisible critic in there too. Your invisible critic works hand in hand with your useful memories, references, and examples and reinforces your belief that something would be dangerous to do. The invisible critic is there to keep us safe, but too many of us allow that critic to hold us back.

Back to choices again. It is up to us who we choose to listen to. If you choose, you can listen to the coach, and they will find all the positive information you need to back you up. Or you choose to listen to the critic, and they will find all the information you need to really put you off.

As you can imagine, the modern virus is pushing us to listen to our critic and to filter out all that is positive and exciting about a healthy dialogue with our coach. If you're tempted to discuss your plans with your nearest zombie, and you manage to get their attention, they will be ready with all the reasons why you shouldn't, can't, and must never stride ahead. One of the many reasons we should not listen to the zombies.

A number of years ago, I was in a bar on a snowboarding trip in Austria. It was not the most memorable of venues. The carpet was sticky, and there was a strange smell in the air. Despite the uninviting environment, I was about to experience something life-changing.

The music in the venue was loud, fast-paced, and pounded a heavy beat. A lonely couple were dominating the dance floor. They were amazing. They moved like two snakes on a hotplate: gyrating, twisting, and turning as though they were part of the same well-oiled machine. The music pulsed them across the floor, and I was transfixed. I wanted that. I wanted to be part of that magic. I had no idea what I was even looking at, but I knew I wanted to be part of it.

There and then I decided I wanted to learn how to dance. On my return home, I announced this to my amazing fiancée and discovered that she too loved the idea of learning to dance. Bolstered by the idea of being safer in numbers, and with positive affirmations from my invisible coach, we went off, found a dance class, and have been dancing ever since. Learning to dance has indeed changed my life. I find it difficult to describe the impact dancing has made on me, my home life, and my business confidence — truly a transformation, and one I am grateful for.

I couldn't have done it without my invisible coach though. If I had *chosen* to listen to my invisible critic, this transformation would not have got off the ground. My critic would have found any excuse to prevent me taking the *risk* or putting in the effort to make it happen.

Dancing, Nick? You? With your two left feet? I don't think so. Not very manly, is it, mate? You're not the most coordinated of people either. Remember that time when...

This is the stuff the critic is there for. Keeping us safe, reminding us of our weaknesses, stopping us making a fool of ourselves, and *holding us back*!

Thank goodness I have a healthy relationship with my invisible coach, and he found all the reasons and references that gave me the encouragement to ceroc, waltz, foxtrot, and line dance my way through the world.

I bring up this story as an example in my workshops quite regularly, and at a recent event, I had a delegate that also wanted to learn how to dance. In fact, his wife was extremely excited about the prospect. I'm sure there are a massive number of partners desperate for an opportunity to release their inner dancer.

So I asked what happened.

He never went through with it. He backed out at the last moment, and that was that.

Why? Because he listened to his invisible critic and focused on all the reasons why it was a bad idea, why it should be avoided, and why he shouldn't go anywhere near any kind of lessons.

His wife was gutted.

So, being the helpful guy I am, I challenged him to have a conversation with his invisible coach and see what he thought. Not surprisingly, the coach was all for it. He had loads of reasons why it was a great idea, how it was possible, and — although frightening — why it was a goal worthy of persistence.

The tide turned, and he decided there and then to make it happen. He was going to book the lessons and surprise his wife when it was all planned. How fabulous is that?

Sometime later, I received an email simply entitled, '*Everyone should learn to dance*', in which he told me he had indeed booked the lessons, they had gone, and they had absolutely loved it. Good work, invisible coach.

Your invisible coach is mighty handy with a metaphorical machete too. As soon as the virus begins to take hold, unleashing your zombie-slaying inner guru is a wise move indeed.

Consider an occasion when you have listened to your invisible coach or critic and explore what was going on. Did you feel the support, see the evidence, and receive the positive affirmation that your coach is ever ready to provide? Or were you bombarded with the negative, the evidence that it was a bad idea and something to avoid, the information that your critic is more than happy to offer you as required?

You want to start a business, ask for a promotion, ask your colleague out on a date, have a challenging conversation with your boss, share how you feel with your partner, train for a marathon, buy a puppy, or learn to scuba dive. Your coach and your critic will be on hand to steer you down the path. They have the same resources, the same information, and rely on the same data bank. Up to you who you choose to listen to.

Zombie or Survivor?

"I am the one not running but facing.
Because if I am the last one, then I am
humanity. And if this is humanity's
last war, then I am the battlefield."
— Rick Yancey, *The 5ᵗʰ Wave*

If we create a healthy relationship with our invisible coach, he/she will become our default resource. Outside of those occasions when our critic will be screaming at us to watch out, to avoid something dangerous (at these points in time both the coach and critic would agree that it is kind of crazy to progress), we will favour the positivity of the coach. This is great news and is to be encouraged in all walks of life. Really stretch yourself. I mean really, really stretch. Dream big and have amazing adventures.

Resilience

Without this healthy relationship with your invisible coach, life either becomes very difficult as you continually beat yourself up over opportunities missed and adventures that pass you by, or it becomes extremely easy as you end up doing nothing, expecting very little and achieving even less — joining the horde in their constant shuffly groans.

I want success, and for me this means progress, striving for exciting goals, and hitting the mark, or getting pretty damn close. To make this a reality takes effort, motivation, and above all, resilience.

Resilience is key.

Running a marathon takes a great deal of training and discipline, but a large part of the race is run in your head, and that is where resilience lives. The ability to keep going and tough it out is an attribute not to be underestimated. Your zombie colleagues struggle to maintain any of this essential hardiness.

Our scale of 1 to 10 that we applied to our self-belief can also be used to measure how resilient we are. Similar scoring applies. 7 and under and you are likely to give up at the first, second, or third hurdle. 8 and 9s leave some 'comfortable' room for doubt to collude with your invisible critic and find a handy excuse to fall short. Only 10 out of 10 resilience gets the race won and the job done.

Self-Belief 10 x Resilience 10 = 100% Ready to Make it Happen

We need to make sure we can turn our 8s and 9s into a 10 for both self-belief and resilience. To do this, we should consider our goal, our target, and our ambition. How hungry are you for it? How worried are you about not making it, and what can we do to enhance both of these factors?

Ravenous Hunger:

Visualise what it will be like when you have made it. The marathon is complete, you have wowed the audience at your conference, you have secured that promotion, or you have pulled off a ceroc triple spin without falling on your backside. What does it look like? How does it feel? How will you celebrate? Who will you tell and share your triumph with? If you can picture all of these things and feel the emotion of success, then you are enhancing that drive, tweaking that desire, and creating a reality that is in tune with your core beliefs.

Horrendous Fear:

What does failure look like? How does not quite making it to the end feel? What are the consequences, now and in the future? You didn't manage to give up smoking, the promotion never came, and you gave up your marathon training and went to the pub instead. It didn't happen, and it will never happen. Who do you share this with? If the idea of failing makes you feel totally rotten and giving up fills you with dread, your resilience is going to fire on all cylinders, and you will see your 10 become a reality.

One of the reasons taking part in a sponsored charity event is a challenge that is more likely to end in success is the fact that you have committed to the adventure and told other people you will succeed. The charity, your sponsors, and your family expect triumph. Quite the motivator and definite fuel in your tank of resilience.

Now I'm not suggesting failure is bad, it could be better, but it is just part of the journey, a hurdle to overcome *as long as you don't give up*. If you fail and your next move is to give up, you are defeated. Your resilience (what's left of it) is beaten, and you have not secured your goal. If you have given it everything you have, and it still hasn't happened, it's time to look for an alternative solution, to ask for help, or to explore other opportunities that bring you similar joy.

Let's plan this together.

Consider a goal that is within your control (a healthy place to start). Mine will be six months off alcohol in 2017 (alternate months starting in January). OK, what's yours? What is big enough to require a self-belief and resilience boost? Have a think and come back to me when you have something that will make a massive difference to you. Don't take too long; the horde is coming, and they will get in your way. The horde come in a variety of shapes and sizes and often wear the disguise of 'helpful' observer. Don't be fooled. These zombies are the naysayers who don't want you to achieve because it makes them feel bad. These are modern cowards who will infect you if you allow them.

What will it take to get your idea on your list? Writing your goals onto a visible list for those nearest and dearest to you to see will really help you stay on track. What additional drivers can you collect to make this challenge (adventure) a reality and one which has both your 10s in place?

I must admit, mine will be a tough challenge; one I can't afford to take lightly. But it's definitely within my control. I need to bolster the likelihood of it working for me, and I need all the help I can get.

My first step was to outline the schedule — pretty straightforward — alternate months starting January 2017. Your schedule will depend on your challenge, but to push your self-belief to a 10, you need to have laser focus and total clarity on when and how the process will take place.

It's going to help massively if you get some support — this will turbo-charge your resilience score. Strangely enough, none of my mates in the pub fancied joining me on this challenge, but there were others that jumped on board with me (at least for the first month).

To give your self-belief and resilience scores the boost they need to secure the 10 spot, you will need to make your challenge worthwhile to you. How will you reward yourself during and after the challenge is complete? What will it mean to you financially, physically, and mentally if you gather momentum and master the journey?

For me, I think I will save the money I would have spent and select something I want to buy, and I'll combine the challenge with a fitness drive, including healthy eating, gym sessions, and plenty of running events. Should all add up to an awesome year. Increased fitness will help me stay ahead of the zombies too, which is a bonus.

I have taken my self-belief from an 8 to a 10, and my resilience will remain at 10 during the additional (bonus) fitness drivers.

At some point, however, it's going to get tough. We're going to wake up and not feel like playing. If it's not tough, perhaps we have set the bar too low after all. This is when we will need to dig deep, call on our coach to give us a gritty pep talk, and look to our supporters for a morale-boosting pick-me-up. We don't have to do it alone. If you are at a loss and your self-belief and resilience are taking a pounding, you can always give me a call. Surround yourself with supporters, those who want the best for you, not the zombies who are just waiting for you to fail and join their horde.

As with most things in life, you have a choice. The decisions are yours to make, and you can decide to head in a positive direction or a negative one.

The zombies are hoping you opt for the negative. They hate to see someone excelling and carving out adventures. It makes them feel bad about their inactivity and lack of belief. The horde bind together and hunger for you to join them.

Be strong, have courage, and dare to be human.

Habits and Challenges

"Life is either a daring
adventure or nothing at all."
— Helen Keller, *The Open Door*

I wonder what February will look like after one month of my challenge. I wonder if this month on month off will become a habit.

What will your challenge look like a month in? Will you be feeling the euphoric energy that comes from achieving step by step progress and success?

I gave up butter, crisps, and chocolate for a year as part of a New Year challenge a few years ago, and after a year, my relationship with those foodstuffs changed to the point that I can take them or leave them. I choose to leave them. It did take a whole year though.

Giving up butter and chocolate was fairly straightforward in comparison to giving up crisps — I sure did love my crisps. Saying no, even now, is sometimes a struggle, and I do like to smell the occasional freshly-opened Easter egg (who doesn't), so the attraction of chocolate is still there.

Most people who set themselves New Year's resolutions do not consider the 10 x 10 factor and are kissing goodbye to their good intentions before the Christmas decorations are back in their box.

The science behind breaking and forming new habits tends to shift. There was a time when I read that it takes twenty-one days to break an old habit or form a new one.

More recently, I read that it actually takes thirty days, and the most up-to-date research suggests sixty-six days of consistent behaviour! Not sure what happened to the habit-breaking population. Perhaps we are weaker than we used to be. This will be the virus reducing our grip on all things that make us human and give us control. Our attention spans are seriously depleted, so this may be having a bearing on how much focus we require to form a new habit. We used to laugh at the poor old goldfish with its minimal memory and attention span. The fish are now laughing at us. Look closely, and you'll see the bubbles rising from their gills.

The science can look after itself. What I find is that some habits are easier than others. Some are going to take a year, some even longer. This is why resilience is a must, and any additional help (internal and external) you can gather could make all the difference.

I like to share my challenges with a number of close friends so they can support and keep an eye on my efforts. I like to think of it as moral support, but it more closely resembles being overseen by the judging panel.

For me, this works.

If you have a challenge that is rather hard-core, then 10 x 10 and a little help from your friends could make all the difference.

Writing to Yourself

Another option that will give you a boost and remind you to stay on track is to provide your own moral support in the form of a letter.

I like to finish my lengthier workshops with an opportunity for my delegates to write to themselves to remind them of the three most important things they have promised to achieve. I put these in the post after a month has gone by to remind them of the changes they need to make and the habits they wish to form.

It's extremely pleasing to receive positive post, and these letters usually come at a time when the busyness of life is encroaching on their good intentions.

Feel free to stop reading right now and write yourself a letter. Give yourself that shot in the arm that may make all the difference when the going gets tough. Say hi, be nice, and have fun.

Imagine you were opening a letter from yourself written six months ago. What do you think it would say? Your response to this should be extremely interesting.

My daughter has written a letter to herself which is designed to be opened when she turns thirty. The letter is vast, written a decade before she turns thirty, and only she knows its contents. I hope the contents prove enlightening and powerful and she celebrates on letter-reading day.

Your Radar

Once you put your dreams and ambitions onto yours and others' radars, your eyes will be wide open for opportunity and the adventures that striving for success bring. This is what radars are for — seeing the target and allowing you to embrace every progressive step.

Build a list, write it down. Is the challenge work related? Have you put a timescale on success? Is it more personal? Have you planned rewards along the way? Is it a major life shift? Do you have the support mechanism in place to keep you on track?

Plan accordingly.

Believe.

My 'radar' currently begins with a whiteboard containing a list of the daily challenges I set myself. Each of these receives a tick as and when they are achieved. The key to my list is the last column which receives a tick only if I have achieved everything on the rest of my list — my 'full on' indicator. The momentum of a series of ticks in this column is incredibly powerful — I must not break the chain.

I have absolute clarity on what I am looking for from my challenges, and this has opened my eyes to a range of other things that are in keeping with my goals. The universe seems to have an eye on my progress and the person I am becoming.

As you progress and hit milestones along the way, you too will become a different version of yourself. You will see the world with new eyes, and your fresh perspective will be revealing. This may take you to brand-new places, physically as well as emotionally, and may present you with opportunities you have never previously considered.

At some point you will look back, prompted perhaps by dated photographs or business milestones, and appreciate how far you have come. These explorations are likely to open your world and put you alongside new people — these will not be the zombies that threaten to put your progress on hold. Embrace all of these adventures because amazing things await.

So you have a recipe to achieve your goals and to strive towards your most important ambitions. Apply your focus through accurate visualisation, take in the wonder of success, and also consider the consequences of failure. Make this application as real as possible. How does it look and how does it feel?

Converse with your invisible coach regularly. Together you can make magic happen.

Add as much help as you can get to influence, inspire, and motivate you to go for it.

10 x 10 (+ some extra lifts along the way) = 100% (and some)

Confronting the Horde and Communicating with Strangers

"Smile at strangers and you just might
change a life." — Steve Maraboli

You never know who you're going to meet at a formal networking event, in a coffee shop, or down the pub.

I attended an event a while ago and met a woman who worked for one of the largest financial institutions on the planet. We chatted and had a fun and informative conversation. Sometime later, after a few more informal exchanges, she introduced me to one of her managers, and we had some more detailed and slightly more formal conversations. These conversations developed, and I had the chance to meet up with her boss. We agreed to do some work together. Over a two-year period and several varied events, I was commissioned to deliver a number of big stage performances at one of their major conferences. A serious stepping stone on my speaking journey. And it all began with a conversation with a stranger.

Once you've got your head around where you are going and you have your invisible coach on your side, the rest of your journey comes down to strategy, technique, and a host of communication skills that can be yours in abundance. The virus continues to spread, but you are ready to be the cure. Your metaphorical machete is sharpened, and you wield it with confidence.

The idea of goal setting permeates through every step on your journey and gives meaning to the adventures. Goals are like the words that appear inside a stick of rock; they are there at the first bite and remain until your last.

Without these objectives firmly fixed in your head and buoyed by self-belief and resilience, communicating with strangers is nothing more than a host of random exchanges.

If we have a goal and a plan, we can turn these contacts into potential collaborations and powerful connections.

Most of your landmark relationships, outside of your immediate family, probably began through chance meetings or interactions with strangers. There's a very good chance that even your relationship with your life partner began as a meeting of strangers at some point.

There are a lot of people out there — not all of them are zombies yet — and it would be a real shame if we didn't explore this broader palette of variety, intrigue, and opportunity.

My younger self would be running scared at this point:

"What do you mean, Nick? Start a conversation with a complete outsider? Run the risk of being ignored, snubbed, or humiliated? No thank you. I'll stick with most parent's advice and never talk to strangers."

Fair enough, younger me; I'm not suggesting we throw caution to the wind and remove common sense. This advice is for us adults.

Stranger Danger

The problem comes when we carry the 'stranger danger' philosophy through into our adulthood. At a reasonably early age, we need to develop the skills to communicate with those we do not know and do it well. It is essential to have effective conversations and explore opportunities and develop meaningful relationships. The virus will continue to make this more of a challenge — but we love a challenge, don't we?

I spoke at an event at a local university recently on all aspects of communication and took a host of questions from the floor so as to really share some value across the most popular topics. Most of the questions were in the area of networking, interviews, and talking to strangers (chatting people up to be more accurate). This is no surprise because most of us come from a childhood where we are immersed in the belief that strangers are dangerous. We are rarely taught (formally) how to transition to an open platform where our ability to get on with new people is a massively valuable skill.

If you were the kind of child that hated to ask questions while at school, would shy away from situations where you could be singled out, and were never picked first when teams were choosing sides, then this transition would have been a difficult one. For some of you, this transition may never have taken place, and it will be holding back not just your career, but many other areas of personal development.

The reason I know this is because I was that shy child and began my working life with very few social skills.

In my early days in business, I remember being at a networking event in Las Vegas — this could and possibly should be the opening of one of the greatest stories ever told. It's Vegas, and there was a free bar around a stunning pool, and the event was packed. Sadly, it is not the greatest story ever told — it may, however, be one of my saddest business tales.

I arrived, and the place was buzzing. The sun was shining, and there were plenty of people having a wonderful time. Like a large number of networking events I attend, if you look at the big picture from the eyes of an 'outsider', it looks like everyone knows everyone else. Everybody looks confident and comfortable and at ease with the world. This is not actually the case. Everyone (bar a few rare exceptions) is as nervous as you. No one knows many people in the room. Everyone is feeling a tad uncomfortable.

Some very wise words I came across many years ago suggest we should:

Never compare how you *feel* on the inside with how other people *look* on the outside.

We can all put a brave face on and muster a sense of confidence even though on the inside we are feeling far from calm. Some of us are better at this than others, but how we appear is not necessarily an accurate indicator as to how we feel.

Chances are the Vegas event was filled with strangers getting to know one another and working through their initial nerves.

I did not know this.

I went to the bar and grabbed a beer and then, sadly, moved to the outside of the group. I do like to observe how people interact, but now wasn't the time to be passive. I watched and waited for someone to interact with me. I must have been sending out magical nervy vibes because there was not a queue of people waiting to make my acquaintance.

I cringe at the situation now because it is so simple to get involved in conversations, and a little courage would have made all the difference.

But, back then, that was not me.

I finished my beer and discretely made my exit, leaving behind adventure, opportunity, and possibly some magical connections.

Back then, I had not made the transition to 'effective communicator', an indispensable skill for any goal-hungry adventurer.

I still see a lack of formal training/teaching for our school-age entrepreneurs in these transitional essentials. Why, I wonder, is 'communicating with the unknown' not a compulsory part of all formal education? When I'm asked to present to a school-age audience, this is the area that is asked about more than any other. When I quizzed a university leader on why networking and communication skills were not a standard part of the learning cycle, his response was that there is no space in the timetable to allocate to this.

I find this difficult to believe. I went to university, and I sat on my backside for hours on end thinking about working and finding myself. I could have squeezed in some additional 'life-changing' lessons.

This 'lack of time' response saddens me. If we refuse to equip our next generation of entrepreneurs with these fundamental zombie-slaying skills, they will struggle to capitalise on their educational qualifications and maximise their career opportunities. It's should be a win-win scenario, but it seems to have missed the educational radar. Our future entrepreneurs seem to be comfortable online but ungainly and awkward face to face.

As a short-term solution, I would suggest passing this book on to any university-age students and encouraging them to digest this section before they embark on their entrepreneurial journey. Let's not miss any opportunities to share our metaphorical machetes.

Getting into a Conversation

What I didn't know at the Vegas networking event was how to easily get into a conversation or how to conduct myself and make the most of the interaction. It's not difficult, and if we're honest, we all know how to enter a conversation (we do it all the time), but I lacked the confidence and technique to even give it a go. I was more zombie than I gave myself credit for.

Pathetic!

Harsh, but true, and I'm not alone in my old lack of proactivity.

First thing's first, when interacting with strangers, try not to approach those in a closed group. I would rather start or join a conversation; I'm not happy butting in, so a closed group is to be avoided. A closed group is tight; there is not really any space between participants to join the throng. The conversation looks intense or secret, and the body language is constricted, heads close and possibly bowed, arms crossed with some localised gestures. Think of a sports huddle. You wouldn't squeeze into one of those unless you had been invited, and a closed group is similar. There is no need to butt in. Be polite: it is an essential skill for the professional networker.

Aim for open groups or people on their own. These are much easier pickings. Open groups have some space between them, a lovely gap for you to slide into. Their body language is more expansive. Their shoulders are turned out, arms open with relaxed gestures.

Approach the open group and say, "*Do you mind if I join you*", and you're in. If you're at a formal networking event, I'd be very surprised if you were turned away — everyone is there to converse, so of course, you are welcome to join.

If you are approaching someone on their own, open with the line, "*Hi, I'm Nick. How are you?*" Feel free to replace my name with your own (if you wish).

If you are approaching a stranger or a group of strangers, and you are not in a place where open networking and conversations are expected, you need to judge the situation and atmosphere professionally.

I tend to begin with a 'Hi' and follow with a comment about the location, environment, or part of the current conversation if this is appropriate.

At a low-key running event at the weekend, I was the only representative from my club and knew no one at the venue. Up to me if I wanted to be social and join in with the others. We can usually be left to our own devices if we send 'leave me alone' zombie body language signals. This is true in most places — except if you are in Ireland, where everyone will want to chat with you because it is such a magical place. I chose not to ignore the presence of others, so I wandered over to join the conversation. A simple comment about the event and I was part of the chat.

Be observant, take in the 'feel' of the situation, and make a positive choice to step up and have a go. People are generally lovely, and you could make an outstanding connection, develop a friendship, fall in love, or find some characters you never want to lay eyes on again for as long as you live. It's all part of the adventure after all.

I was in a coffee shop recently, and sitting opposite was a young woman busy writing in her notebook. She had a new, unopened notebook to one side. I'm a big fan of a fresh notebook, something about the anticipation of filling it with magical content, and I was enjoying the bustle and aromas of the vibrant location. I simply mentioned the excitement of the unopened book to the young woman, whose name was Abigail, and a brief conversation began.

We both had a 'live event' interest, and I gave her my card when she asked so she could explore my background in more detail. Will something come of this? Will I receive a call out of the blue to book me for a speaking engagement? Who knows? That's the beauty of communicating with strangers; you never know what will happen. The chances of this particular connection developing into a business relationship is more likely now we've had a conversation.

When was the last time you could have opened a conversation but chose to remain silent? I'm not suggesting we jabber on with anyone who passes us and become that person people cross the street to avoid. But sometimes there are opportunities just waiting to be unearthed — they just take a little digging, and you have a verbal shovel at your disposal. Give it a go. Let's say once in the next week, get your shovel out and see what happens. If you like it, up the ante and step up to twice a week. You'll soon be discovering treasure in more places than you could have imagined.

I was once in a queue in the post office and had a thought-provoking communication experience. It was a busy and rather stuffy atmosphere, and there was quite a line. I snailed my way to the head of the queue, and just in front of me was a young woman with a toddler who would not stand still. The youngster was wonderfully distracted by all the post office paraphernalia and merchandise. When the mum came to pay for the numerous parcels she was posting, it became obvious all was not well. She was hunting through her purse and becoming more and more agitated. It transpired that her 'little darling' had been playing with her credit cards, and they had not made their way back into her possession! She only had one card (which the post office would not accept) and no cash, oh dear.

I know what it's like to have kids. I've been waiting in line with bored toddlers, and I'm aware that they communicate with no regard to their surroundings, your feelings, or with any social grace. It's a tough enough job, raising kids, without them sabotaging your post office transactions.

I couldn't stand by and let the mum take back all of the parcels only to have to repeat the undesirable queuing experience when she had recovered her cards, so I stepped forward and offered to pay. It was a random act of kindness that I would like to think would be repeated if someone I knew was in a similar dilemma.

The lady was extremely grateful and insisted we go to the bank and, using the only card in her possession, withdraw some money to pay me back. I was happy with her offer, although didn't expect it.

On our way to the bank, we chatted about a number of things, and it turned out she worked in the publishing industry and would be a superb contact for my daughter. I gave her my card, and she promised to be in touch with some information that would assist my daughter in her career pursuits.

To this day, I've never heard from her. We did go to the bank, and she paid me back, but she never followed up on her suggestion of supplying some information.

Does this mean I should not bother in future? Am I a fool to expect people to follow up on their promises? I don't think so. My expectations are realistic, and I like to trust that people will do their best.

I have no idea why the information did not appear as pledged. It could be any number of reasons from simple forgetfulness, technological interference, or perhaps her magpie of a son took a shine to my card as well. Let's hope the zombies didn't get her. We'll never know, but given a similar opportunity again, I will continue to opt for the human communication and provide help wherever possible.

You never know what will transpire, maybe nothing, but maybe something truly phenomenal will happen.

Get into conversations with strangers often. It is where magic happens.

Networking vs the Zombies

"There are two types of people. Those
we who come into a room and say,
"Well, here I am!" and those who come
in and say, "Ah, there you are.""
— Frederick Collins

I network a lot and have met countless people on my travels. I have assisted a huge number of them in a variety of positive ways. If you have the courage to communicate with a stranger, you are opening the door to another world, a progressive environment where success lives and adventures await.

Say 'Hi' to the next stranger you come across. Be kind, be human, and be authentic. Awesome! They may not expect it, and you could witness the virus lifting from their view. This is not as easy as it used to be. The virus has us focusing on our mobile devices and not aware of the world around us. Your next 'stranger' may be a little surprised that you are talking to them.

One of the ways to ensure you are approachable and maximise your time with strangers at networking events is to adopt a 'host' mindset. Just imagine everyone has been invited to your party. You are their cordial host, and you want them all to have a fabulous time. Let's get this party started! Come on you zombies, welcome aboard.

Just like being a formal host, you are responsible for making early introductions, pairing newcomers with others who they have something in common with, and making sure everyone's basic needs are met. At a formal networking event, this puts you in the centre of the action.

At a recent event, I was enjoying working my way from conversation to conversation. Having listened well, I was able to identify if I had already met someone who would be a useful contact for those I was currently with. It wasn't difficult. If I came across a valuable connection, I made it a priority to introduce them to whoever was a meaningful contact in the room, and then I would leave them to it. It didn't take long before people were coming up to me to see if I knew a whole raft of potential connections. It was a very streamlined way to cover a great deal of ground, and I met more than my fair share of networkers.

If you are communicating with strangers in an environment that is not a formal networking event, use your powers of observation, coupled with active listening, to position your 'inner host'. You will soon know if introductions are appropriate.

Conversations are easier to get into if you allow yourself to shine. Playing the host is one of the ways you can shine bright.

Another, not recommended, way to 'shine' or certainly bring attention to yourself is to cause a scene. Not what you are looking for in most situations, but I have known it work really well (although it was by accident). I was at an event in a car showroom: sixty guests in close proximity enjoying a glass of complimentary wine. The gentleman I was speaking with accidentally dropped his wine glass onto the shiny and solid floor. Smash! Such a loud noise for a small piece of glass. The room instantly went quiet as though it was all about to 'kick off', and all heads turned in our direction.

Everyone was poised, silent, and a little embarrassed for my clumsy companion. What an opportunity to introduce yourself and your company at that point!

A large proportion of my business comes, both directly and indirectly, from people I meet at networking events. The biggest stage appearance I have made to date began as a conversation within a networking group. On the flip side, many of my suppliers have come from networking environments. They are a place where business develops, not directly or straight away, but over time. With the right ingredients, networking provides a mass of opportunities.

You have to work at it and make the most of the opportunities that this environment sends your way.

Recently, I attended a formal networking event, and one of the guests had an announcement to make to the group as a whole. This is pretty standard for a formal event, and a superb opportunity to advertise to a captive audience. The announcement was to promote a forthcoming workshop for any business that had employees. The dates and locations were announced with enthusiasm, and the message reached a natural conclusion. Job done.

Not quite. What the presenter failed to mention was what the workshop was about! Unless you were aware of these workshops before the announcement, you would have no clue as to the topic and, hence, have no reason to attend. It's a bit like saying, "There's a TV show on later. Would you like to watch it?" The critical part of the message was missing. The most worrying thing, from my perspective, was that no one in the audience of seventy people mentioned that the crucial detail had been omitted. I didn't mention it either as I knew the person in question and didn't want to embarrass her while she was doing her best to make the broadcast.

Sometimes we are so fixed on the delivery of our message that we leave out the reason we need to make the announcement in the first place. This is especially true when communicating with strangers. We are so focused on what we want to say that we either miss some key detail from the other person's conversation, or we lose our purpose in cordial conversation.

We've all been there. Someone is talking to us, sharing their best information, and we're interested in what *we* are going to say next. Our stuff is so good that we focus on what's coming next, how we are going to respond, and what gems we are going to share. So inwardly focused are we, that the other person's conversation is lost — oops. What was it they were talking about? Too late to zone back in, just nod and say yes and hope that will do.

This is both embarrassing and extremely human. Listening is so much more difficult than hearing. You must focus to really listen, and it takes a healthy amount of concentration. Failure to properly listen will put you first in line for the zombie buffet. It may be easy to hide behind the hectic mix of communication busyness, but failure to keep your ears and your eyes open will ensure you are surrounded by the horde.

Pitch Your Opening Conversation to Wake the Undead

"A good conversationalist is not one
who remembers what was said, but says
what someone wants to remember."
— John Mason Brown

Throughout our communication journey, we are looking to achieve a series of goals. These may be as simple as pleasant and interesting dialogue, chats that are entertaining and informative, or it may be more focused and targeted on a business/personal development objective.

In a *networking* environment (networking comes in many forms, but I would like to separate it from social communication), it is important to communicate in a way that maximises your opportunities.

To capitalize on your interaction, you need to focus on a series of tasks.

Firstly, ask the other person/people what it is they do. And listen. Listen hard. Work at this, be interested, ask questions, and show that you care. Listen with your ears and your eyes and ensure you take on board any area where you may be able to add value and help them out.

At my most recent networking event, I chatted with a business owner who could add immense value to another contact of mine who was in the room at the time. An easy introduction and an excellent connection potentially developed. This was only possible through active listening and some targeted questioning. I uncovered a set of services I knew would be of interest because I had previously listened to my other contact and was able to join the dots.

During your conversation, make sure you ask who really powerful contacts for them would be. If the ideal connection was in the room, who would that be? Ask them to be as detailed and specific as they can. This way, we can visualise their ideal client, which serves us in two valuable ways. Firstly, it makes it easy for us to identify if we know any contacts that match their ideal customer type, and it gives us some useful information to enable an easy exit from the conversation. One of the questions I am asked most with regards to networking is how to exit from a conversation. The details of this simple exit strategy are on their way.

What to Say?

When given your moment in the limelight, I suggest we allow ourselves to shine first.

If you are conversing with someone who is pleasant and polite, I would expect them to also take an interest in you and ask what it is you do (or something similar if you are not at a formal networking event). You will come across plenty of people who are only interested in talking about themselves, and more often than not, they have nothing of any real interest to say. It's mighty tedious. I remember a horror of a networker who shimmied his way through the crowd, leading with his business card, and infecting everyone in his path with his bad manners, bad breath, and glibly suggesting 'we catch up soon' to each and every victim. In the world of networking, they are referred to as a *shark* (I prefer *zombie* or possibly *tosser*).

Let's assume you are with someone who is not an Olympic bore and is actually human. You need to be prepared to work your magic. Here is your opportunity to begin a potentially sensational relationship, so let's do it well.

Let them know what you do based on what you deliver for your clients; this is rarely your job title. Think for a moment what value you bring to your customers. What it is you do for them to take away their headaches, make their business run smoother, and their lives less complicated.

Have a think. Too often I have heard an accountant at a networking event announce that 'I'm just an accountant' as though that was all there was to be said. All you accountants out there, you are so much more than that.

The virus will have you opting for the obvious: a standard, horde-like response. Fight this.

Your job title only tells me a superficial amount of information (in most cases). Think a little deeper and consider what your clients would say you do. Ask yourself what happens if you do an amazing job. What are your clients left with? What happens if it goes horribly wrong? What does that look like? From here you will have a better idea as to what it is you do to make the former a reality and to minimise the chances of the worst happening.

Although I run a training company, I rarely lead with that information.

I assist teams and individuals to enhance how they communicate so they can achieve greater success. I help my clients to communicate with more power

than they ever thought possible, and I help organisa-
tions to slay their zombies.

Always be ready and happy to give more detail and provide examples and anecdotes of where your work has had a huge impact. If you have listened closely to your companion, you can share a story that relates to their industry.

Your opening couple of sentences will take some crafting, but once you're happy, it will open up more doors and give the listener the best chance to see your 'beneath the surface' value.

I once heard a networker introduce himself by saying that he *'shoots people and blows them up!'* It turned out he was a photographer. With some professions, in some groups, that kind of quirk can have a healthy impact. I have also worked with a physiotherapist who networks predominantly with doctors, so his introduction is far more in keeping with the professional standards of medical circles. He starts by introducing himself as a physiotherapist and then adds some specific value based on his particular skill set.

Whatever it is you 'do', be ready to communicate your *value* and what your ideal clients 'look' like. Share it with enthusiasm and make it as easy as possible for those around you to see why this is important and how you, and your work, make it so much better/stronger/quicker/easier/safer/more profitable/more fun etc.

Share with them how it feels, what it looks like, and why you are the magic ingredient in the mystical soup that is your industry.

Give them an example or share an anecdote based on a recent client interaction. If you tell me a story, I am so much more likely to understand and see exactly where you are coming from.

Now you are networking like a professional.

There is room now for a bit of a chat. If you are at a formal networking session, this does not need to be too extensive but detailed enough to see if you have common interests, areas of similarity, and if you like the sound of the person you are communicating with. In other words, would you like to get to know them better and do business with them if the occasion presented itself?

You need to work hard to speak to a number of networking strangers at each event you visit, so your conversations cannot be drawn-out affairs.

If you are not at a formal networking event, you can chat for as long as you wish. Share some stories and buy a latte/beer.

Conversing with strangers is a dying art replaced by Facebook comments, Twitter hashtags, Snapchat stories, and numerous other social media interactions. Conversations have become global and virtual — there is value in that, but we should not allow it to replace the power of a face-to-face exchange. It's far too easy to allow the virus to dominate our *social* communication and turn genuine interaction into the churning of content.

Face to face opens the doors to real connections and relationships. Meet, converse, and make magic happen.

Once the conversation has run its course, or you need to exit the exchange (as there's a room full of other people to mix with), you need to get out of the conversation in a professional and polite way.

This is not as difficult as it seems, and this technique can be used to extricate yourself from any conversation.

When the moment is right, simply use the past tense. For example, "*It's been lovely speaking with you*". Conclude by suggesting you will look out for any other networkers who would be excellent connections for them.

> "*It's been great speaking with you, Alan. If I come across any sales managers who are looking to develop their team, would you like me to introduce you? No problem. Have an excellent rest of your evening.*"

I use this a lot. Psychologically, we understand that the past tense means the conversation is drawing to a close, and when followed up with a positive, the exchange should conclude in an upbeat manner.

Don't forget that networking is all about helping one another, so if you have promised to assist someone, please ensure you make good on your undertaking.

In brief, a summary of professional networking looks like this:

- Get into a conversation
- Ask them what they do
- Listen and comment. Can you help them?
- Introduce what you do and back it up with an example (as relevant as possible)
- Chat about stuff — explore common interests
- Get out of the conversation
- Fulfil your promises

It's not that challenging, but so many people do it badly. There really is no excuse. Be polite, be interested, and be interesting, and see what adventures await.

It also helps to have a strategy. Zombies don't.

Zombies tour from event to event, one potential interaction after another, making no actual progress. They have no focus, just shuffling through the groups, groaning. They will keep coming back while there are weak targets to infect, but they won't make the lasting impression that the professionals do. You must have more focus than this.

What is it you are looking to achieve from your networking experience? If you don't know, then stop and think. It pays to be as specific as you can on your goals.

If you don't know what your ideal clients look like, how will anyone you come across know what they look like? I have lost count of the people who respond to the question, *'Who would be really good connections for you?'* with, *"Oh, anyone with a budget"* or, *"Anyone with plenty of staff"*. Too vague, too weak, and of no use whatsoever! Join the queue of zombies heading nowhere.

How on earth am I supposed to help? The pool of possible connections is too wide, too deep, and too cold for me to venture into. Warm it up, narrow it down, and make it easy for me to spot.

Know who the best type of clients/connections are before you go anywhere near your next networking event. Ideally, I would like you to be so clear that you can refer to examples by name.

What do they do, what industries are they in, what problems do they have that you solve, what do they look like? Narrow, narrow, narrow so they are easier to identify and spot.

For example, great connections for me are financial organisations who have a team of customer-facing representatives who are currently undergoing change and facing increased pressure to perform better with little or no additional resources. What they look like are relationship managers for banking institutions or financial advisers attached to larger commercial organisations.

Do you know any of these? Chances are you can answer that question with much more focus and clarity than if I asked you to let me know of anyone who has a budget. If you don't know any relationship managers or financial advisers, that's OK. But if you did, and I failed to ask effectively, that would be an opportunity missed.

Presence is Your Gift

"We convince by our presence, and to
convince others we need to convince
ourselves." — Amy Cuddy

One of the strategies that will help you in a room full of strangers and will allow you to communicate with more power in any scenario is authoritative body language.

Think for a moment of those individuals and personalities who have outstanding self-assurance. They stand out from the crowd; there is just something about them that puts them a shoulder above the rest. This is *presence*. It's not too difficult to spot: the head is held high, the shoulders are back, there is a smile on their face, and they are totally in the moment, focused, concentrating, and oozing eye contact. We can all do this, which is great news. Very few of us actually do though, which is a shame.

When you're feeling at your best, you are totally unstoppable, on fire with energy, enthusiasm, and can achieve most things. Even those around you during this euphoric and animated part of the journey can expect to be carried along by the magnetism. If, however, you are struggling (I do from time to time. I'm as human as the next guy and have to battle the virus), you will be hesitant, lack positivity, and will feel the energy seeping out of your ideas. It's tough but definitely worth striving to be the best version of yourself.

You choose?

Yep.

You'll recognise the truth in this. There are times when you are outstandingly awesome — loving life to the full. And there will be times when it's all a little bit shit!

You can choose which *you* is let loose on the world.

First, breathe deep. Stand tall. A little taller. Smile. Shoulders back. Smile some more. Make those around you wonder what you've been up to. Remember the times you were totally awesome, and say to yourself, "I choose to be awesome".

Now say it out loud.

I choose to be awesome.

Don't forget your invisible coach is in there and on your side. He or she (or it) knows you're phenomenal and has references and memories at the ready. Trust in your coach to support you.

Any of those individuals you considered earlier, those with self-confidence, will be experts at this exercise. The more you choose to be awesome, the easier it will become. Why would you choose the alternative?

Life is all about choices. You always have a choice. You get to choose how you react to any situation. The outcome may not always be what you're looking for, but you get to choose what you do about that too. Do you sit back and take it, or do you do something about it?

Presence is a combination of positive body language and your inner awesomeness. Don't slouch, don't mumble, and don't avoid eye contact. Be in your zone, concentrate, and give it your best.

Dr Amy Cuddy is leading the field in the study of presence, and her wonderful TED Talk will give you superb insights to the science behind mastering your inner superhero.

In a networking environment, your inner awesomeness is highly attractive and will give you the edge over your competition. Be present, smile, and embrace the adventure.

Open for Business and More

"She has lost the art of conversation,
but not, unfortunately, the power of
speech." — George Bernard Shaw

Communicating with strangers is easier if you work towards an 'open' conversational style. This is a relaxed, calm approach with softer gestures and open body language. We're asking lots of insightful questions because we are listening well, and we are interested in the stranger. We nod appropriately, empathise by smiling and tilting the head slightly to indicate our concern and understanding, and we are totally in the moment. This is a natural state by the way, not an act. The more we are in the moment, the more we will recognise this approach.

If we lose focus, we will soon be back to drifting out of a conversation. Before we know it, we've stopped listening and have missed some crucial information along the way. Back to nodding and agreeing to something you haven't properly heard. Stop doing that! Zombies have perfected this.

We have entered an age where it seems to be more and more difficult to stay in the moment. We are surrounded by the busy noise of everyday communication, and our attention span has shrunk. The virus is not helping here, and we are finding it more and more difficult to maintain our levels of concentration.

Don't forget, the goldfish is currently giving you a run for your money in the attention stakes.

We are evolving, and this means we need to work a little harder to stay focused and in the moment.

This is a serious communication issue. Partners are not listening to each other because the TV is on in the background. Work colleagues are missing essential signals because they're writing emails while on the phone. Parents are not truly hearing what their children are trying to say because they are checking updates on their device. Kids are no longer in touch with their parents because they communicate best on multiple platforms which are still foreign and move too fast for much of the older generation.

In a networking environment, people are distracted by who else is in the room (who was that I saw out of the corner of my eye?) and by the obsession of working out what they're going to say next.

STOP IT!

When my daughter was very young, we were out for a journey in her buggy, and as a bee buzzed past her, she remarked, *'what was that I almost saw?'*, which still makes me smile some twenty years later. Little did I know at the time that this was to become the underlying current of modern communication.

What was that you almost saw?

Be present. Pay attention. Stop what you're doing and listen. Properly. No excuses.

Multi-tasking is a myth. You can't really concentrate fully on the conversation if your head is somewhere else. Turn off all your mobile notifications. Better still, put your mobile device in your bag, turn it off, and forget about it. You don't need it right now. Let it go. Let it go. Let it go.

Be open to what the other person is saying, absorb their message, and respond proactively to their content.

Paying Attention?
Name Your Rewards

"It's not how big your pencil is;
it's how you write your name."
— Dave Mustaine

One of the benefits of being totally present is the opportunity to remember the names of the strangers you have communicated with. This is a skill that pays huge dividends but is practised by very few networkers. Ever come across a modern zombie that could remember more than a handful of names? Zombies are poor at this basic but essential skill.

I often hear people say they are terrible with names as though that is an excuse for instantly forgetting the name of the person they are talking to.

I'm sure we've all been in that awkward position of hearing a name and promptly losing it again in the conversation. It's really embarrassing if you are asked who you were speaking with, and you simply can't recall their name. Rather unprofessional too.

We're only human though, and we have a lot on our plates. If you lead a busy life, there is only so much you can take on board on a daily basis... Zombie alert!

This sounds like a throwaway excuse to me. A typical response for those among us who are too lazy to concentrate at a time when we should be concentrating most. Is this a symptom of the virus, an early warning sign?

Confusion about a name is acceptable. Hearing it and filing it away in the 'not important/never going to use that' section of your brain is not.

A couple of weekends ago, I was running with a colleague from my running club, and we were chatting about all manner of things. We have talked on a number of occasions over a year or so, and he is among approximately 200 people who regularly run with the club. At one point during the run, he apologised for not being sure of my name. Is it Mark or Martin? "Good try. It's Nick", I told him and then proceeded to call him John, at which point he corrected me and reminded me he was called Pete. What a couple of fools we must have looked. But, out of 200 people, it is understandable that there may be some crossover leading to a comedy sketch moment like this one.

In a networking environment, there is no excuse. You ask someone who they are, they tell you, and you immediately forget. Are we really that busy?

To remember names, you need to care. You have to pay attention and concentrate and commit the name to memory. I find it really useful to use the name as early and as often as I can (within reason) so it sticks in my head. It also pays to visualise any other person you already know who shares the same name and superimpose their features onto the stranger in front of you at the time.

Add a bit of spice to that visualisation, and you can begin to bolt on any other pertinent piece of information to this 'character' you are creating. With a little imagination, you should be able to remember their name, their job, and detail regarding family and hobbies.

So my running partner the other Sunday now has a number of imagined additions to his visage. I have another friend called Pete who owns a small dog and rides a 60s-style scooter. My running companion is now imagined riding the same with a dog on one shoulder. On his other shoulder is an image of two identical women in wedding dresses because we had a discussion about his daughter who has been married twice, to the same guy — an interesting story indeed.

Ideally, when I next see Pete, all these images should spring to mind, and my memory will be on my side to enhance the relationship and future conversations.

The art is to commit this information to memory quickly so you can concentrate on the conversation and how you may be able to assist. Practise this. Try it out on people you know and build a rapid picture. Piece together memorable information about the person to get a feel for the method, so you are ready to have some fun and apply it to strangers, connections, and acquaintances.

You don't want to lose yourself during this process, so practise is a real help. There are other things going on during your conversations with strangers that you can't afford to miss either.

Reading the Signals

"To acquire knowledge, one must
study; but to acquire wisdom, one must
observe." — Marilyn Vos Savant

Other than asking the bold question, 'How does that feel?', the best way to read the emotional response from a stranger during a conversation is by taking notice of their body language.

Much has been written (there are volumes of books on the subject) about non-verbal communication, and it is far from an exact science, but a basic grounding in what is going on inside someone's head is very powerful indeed.

Let's explore what might be going on by observing some typical body language behaviour. We'll investigate how to ensure our body language adds power to our words later in the book. For now, it's all about spotting clues to get inside the heads of some strangers.

Look into My Eyes

Eye contact is a must when dealing with strangers. Our virus-induced colleagues are shockingly bad at giving eye contact. Picture your nearest zombie. Where are their eyes? What are they focusing on? Are they looking in your direction? I very much doubt it; they are obsessed with anything that isn't human.

Good quality eye contact is a direct signal that we are interested, we are following the other person's train of thought, and we are sincere, which is handy, especially if we are looking to build rapport.

When eyes begin to drift, relationships begin to shift.

In other words, if you lose it, you lose it. Without healthy eye contact, it is very difficult to build trust. If you're mid-conversation and your partner's eyes drift off to someone else in the room, that can't be a good sign. If the eyes come straight back to you, take that as a signal you may not be the most interesting person in the room, but you're doing OK.

If we are maintaining decent eyeballs, not only will we be sending positive signals, but we will also be ready to spot other key body language signals as they occur.

Tiny is Worthy

To spot the micro-expressions of others requires us to be focused and attentive. A micro-expression is a reliable reaction to new information, such as elevated eyebrows when shocked or surprised or a furrow in the brow when we disagree or are concerned about what has just been said. These are really useful because they tell us what the other person *feels* about our conversation without them having to say a word.

Our dead-eyed competition is never going to spot any of these useful momentary signals.

When you first meet someone, it is worth looking out for an 'eyebrow flash', a micro-expression in the form of raised eyebrows which lasts only a moment but is usually a sign they are pleased to see you — a very good sign indeed. Don't confuse the eyebrow flash with a signal of raised eyebrows accompanied by a wide-eyed look. This possibly means they are surprised to see that you're still alive!

The more we observe, the more we will begin to see, and our repertoire of micro-expression understanding will build. As body language is not an exact science, we should be looking for clusters of responses rather than individual (one-off) indications. If someone crosses their arms, for example, this doesn't necessarily mean you are beginning to bore them, or they are feeling defensive, but it could do. Look for other body language signals such as leaning back, foot tapping, steam coming out of the ears. When added together, you should be able to read the situation with some accuracy.

To Extremities and Beyond

It's typically the extremities that give us away. Our head, our hands, and even our feet will betray us and give away clues as to how we are feeling.

This is referred to as 'emotional leakage', our emotions seeping out of us through our hands and feet.

Zombies know this, so they shuffle their feet, leaving nothing to chance, keeping their heads down and hands limp by their sides. Zero emotion, zero leakage, zero interest too.

You will often observe people shuffling their feet when they are uncomfortable; children regularly pivot one foot from side to side when they are being selective with the truth. Networkers inadvertently show they are ready to move on by pointing their feet away from our conversation (and often towards the door). When talking about relationships, see how many people play with their wedding rings. If someone is nervous, you can watch them wringing their hands as the nervous energy finds its release. Ladies, you tend to play with your jewellery when you're feeling uncomfortable, and us gents have a habit of putting our hands in our pockets and playing with our change (hopefully it's the change we're jingling). Pretty distracting and speaks volumes.

If we pay attention and observe effectively, we can do something with this *additional* information. Up to you how you choose to react, but we are now communicating from a position in which we are more informed. We have an edge and can respond appropriately depending on how we want the conversation to develop.

One of the reasons online *conversations* leave us feeling struck with the virus is their lack of these essential emotional responses.

If you find your conversation is not engaging enough (I know, it's rare. We are all fabulous people to be around), you can act on the inevitable drifting of eye contact. Try changing direction and ask a number of questions to re-engage the other person and get them talking. We generally want to hear much more from them, so a lack of eye contact is a timely reminder that it is their turn to share some magic.

Appropriate Touching

When I notice a good deal of nervous energy (restless hands, shuffling feet, chattering teeth), I will work hard to reassure. I'll talk in softer tones, tilt my head, and even engage with some appropriate touching.

What! You touch strangers?

Oh yes.

Appropriate touching.

Talking about this tends to freak people out a little. Doing it doesn't, but talking about it does. Weird, huh?

I ran a workshop recently, and the topic was discussed. There were such mixed responses that the subject was dropped for future workshops of that kind. Such anti-touch passion runs high in some circles, which is a shame.

We are talking about occasional, reassuring, and re-affirming touches that are always appropriate and brief. For example, a light pat on the upper arm or shoulder is incredibly powerful.

Use this to reassure, to reinforce a message, and to bond with a possible connection or potential client.

We shake hands on a regular basis, so we shouldn't be afraid of some very gentle, appropriate contact of other kinds.

In Richard Wiseman's book *Quirkology*, he talks about a paper written by Crusco and Wetzel in which two waitresses were trained to appropriately touch diners (shoulders or palm) for exactly one and a half seconds as they passed them their bill. This touching exercise produced bigger tips than those with a *hands-off* approach, supporting the theory that we don't mind a little touchy-feely magic[5].

I'm not suggesting we get carried away and hug our way through a networking event, and you really need to be able to judge when physical contact is fitting, but a human

---

5   *Quirkology* by Richard Wiseman, 2007; A. H. Crusco & C. G. Wetzel – 'The Midas Touch: The effects of interpersonal touch on restaurant tipping', 1984

connection of this kind can go a long way to building an effective bond.

The zombies are going to hate this. Anything that re-affirms our human bond will meet with groans from the horde.

Non-Verbal Cues

All of this *non-verbal* behaviour can be interpreted, sometimes well and sometimes poorly. Ideally, look for clusters of activity which seem to tell you how the other person is feeling and how they have taken your information on board. Don't rely on just the one signal as there are usually numerous reasons why we use non-verbal communication.

Some of the signs to look out for as part of these useful body language clusters are:

- A lack of eye contact — rarely a good sign, shows a possible lack of interest or an absence of trust. This kind of distraction is cause for concern.
- Frowning when the words used seem to be favourable — there could be some anxiety under the surface that's worth exploring.
- Head tilt — usually a sign of empathy, but can be an indicator of condescension, especially when accompanied by a hushed sigh.
- Shaking of the head (side to side) — standard disagreement gesture, but if it accompanies supportive words, something is probably up.
- Tightening of lips — possibly an indicator that the other person is holding their tongue and has an issue with your side of the discussion.

- A non-genuine smile (one that doesn't travel up the face to the corners of the eyes) — could be a placatory gesture that lacks the sincerity your discussion requires.
- Playing with jewellery, hair, or touching the neck/face — usually indicates that the other person is uncomfortable. This could be for any number of reasons, but it's worth exploring.
- Wringing of hands, fiddling with rings, scratching, playing with belt/buttons etc. — these are all indicators that the '*teenage spiders*' are running riot. Your hands can be such an asset, but if you don't know what they're up to (just like teenagers), they're likely to let you down (more on this later).
- Feet tapping/swivelling — is usually a sign of impatience or unrest.
- Feet pointing away from you — typically indicates the direction of travel the other person is eager to take. Feet pointing towards you, usually a good sign. Pointing away, something may be up. They could easily be pushed for time, so look for other indicators to support your thinking.

This is by no means an exhaustive list, so take this as a rough guide. As a general rule of thumb, when something feels wrong and your intuition pokes you in the ribs and says, 'hold on a second', there is probably something amiss. It would be dangerous to read too much into the situation without taking a mental step back and considering the bigger picture. Slow down, observe, and act accordingly. The zombies won't know what hit them.

Building Relationships — Phone Call Fridays

"Saying what we think gives a wider
range of conversation than saying what
we know." — Cullen Hightower

One strategy I have seen great success with is 'phone call Friday'. In our world of connected technology and infinite content, it is becoming increasingly difficult to get through to our audience. Especially as the virus spreads from home to home, office to office, and infects even the most sacred of our domains.

We all receive a ridiculous amount of emails every day. It's the go-to answer for most office zombie communicators. Very few of these emails are requested or welcome but still, they continually rain into mine, yours, and everyone else's digital devices. Sadly, your inbox is a to-do list that the entire world has access to.

Email, in its current format, is no longer an effective method of communicating because of the sheer volume of 'noise' that we have to wade through every time we open our email application. The next generation is already moving on to more effective methods of being heard.

During a recent talk to university students, I explored the current use of email, and they were not fans. Given the choice, they would opt for a host of alternatives.

Why is it we feel as though we couldn't communicate if we didn't have email? The truth is likely that we would communicate far better.

Psychologists have found that our constant checking for the arrival of new mail is feeding the same part of our brains rewarded when we play fruit machines. If you have ever played what used to be called a 'one-armed bandit', you will know that every few spins of the reels will result in some form of reward. It is the same with our emails. Every few 'spins', the mail we receive will contain something of interest. I say 'interest' in its weakest sense as most emails contain something salesy or distracting. But still, we check. Waiting for our reward, again and again and again.

This should be cause for concern. Some people become addicted to fruit machines…

The zombies love their email, so it's here to stay — for a while anyway.

Like junk mail that used to pour through your letterbox, email is steadily becoming more of a problem than a tool to assist your communication journey.

One of the strategies to receive less email is to send less out in the first place. I like this idea. If we are going to send less mail, then we will have an opportunity to do things differently.

Phone call Friday is (like most things communication) not difficult. It's a step back to the 'old days' before email ruled the world. The plan is to have a day (for me it's Friday) where you send no emails. By all means, receive the standard few hundred, but don't be tempted to send any. Instead, pick up the phone.

It's amazing what will happen. Firstly, people will be surprised to receive the call. The phone is your 'secret' weapon.

Who makes phone calls any more? Not that many people, as it turns out. We are too busy writing emails to each other.

Be prepared for your world to be turned around, to find out some incredible things, to laugh, to bond, and to connect on a deeper level. Emails rarely deliver any of these things. Research from Yahoo Labs and the University of California found that the average email response consisted of no more than five words! In no way is that a conversation.

Go on, stop for a moment, pick up the phone (it's never far away), and ring someone you haven't seen for a while. Say hello and share a little magic. Then come back to the book with a smile on your face.

Wake a few zombies with a surprising phone conversation.

After a networking event, you want to continue the momentum of the initial meeting, and this means connecting with those you have met as soon as you can as part of your follow-up strategy. Seriously consider the phone for this if appropriate — no one else will be doing this, so you will have both a considerable impact and the edge over your competition.

Ownership!

"Freedom begins the moment you
realize someone else has been writing
your story and it's time you took the
pen from his hand and started writing it
yourself." — Bill Moyers

Your success when communicating with strangers is linked to how much you care. It's another choice you can make. If you don't care, then don't be surprised if the connections you make do not develop into relationships. If you listen, focus, and follow up on your promises, you are in great shape for developing connections and profitable relationships.

It's up to you, so be in the driving seat, and own the direction of your communication.

Social/Business Events

Most of what we have explored is based on your communication with strangers in a business environment. If you are interacting with strangers in a social capacity, then most of the information still holds true, but you can afford to tone down the formality until it fits the circumstances.

We are naturally social beings, so the informal interactions, in theory, should be much easier. If, however, you struggle with the unknown and aren't ready to share your magic with the world, then apply the business networking strategies and tune them to your personality.

Flexible or Authentic?

To what degree is your communication style, technique, and language choice shaped by the environment you find yourself in? Does your approach fall into the 'flexible' bracket? Is this affecting your authenticity?

I used to find that my communication style was different if I was down the pub to when I was in a formal networking environment. It was still very me, but it was a different '*shade*' of me, a flexible me. It was like I was wearing a different set of clothes for each occasion. Some environments called for jeans and others a suit. My communication style would morph to suit the situation.

This is extremely normal. I was comfortable with this for a long time. It was quite a shock to explore the healthy alternative and to investigate which version of me was the real and authentic one.

Authenticity is an absolute must if you truly want to get through to your audience, but flexibility is still considered useful. There is a fine line between flexibility and being inauthentic though, and our digital, zombie-filled world is pushing us over this line, and that's not great for long-term communication.

Authentic communication is rare, and this makes it oh so powerful.

Consider those people you totally respect. Those you look up to, would follow, invest in, and support through thick and thin. Do these people communicate with utmost authenticity? Now consider those people who are overtly *flexible*, who turn it on and spin accordingly, who have questionable morals, and are focused on number one. Are these the people who inspire you?

What version of you appears on your CV? Is this flexibility or inauthenticity? The zombie social media posts lack the levels of accuracy that stimulates a tangible level of trust.

It does make me smile when people I know transform into a completely different version of themselves when immersed into an unusual situation. We all know people who have a posh voice for addressing strangers. There is a fine line between shaping yourself according to your environment, putting on a show, and being truly you. Authenticity becomes far more comfortable the more courageous you are. As you battle the horde, it will be empowering to wear your authentic self with pride and deliver your unique brand of impact.

I work hard to be authentic wherever I am. At work, at home, and beyond, you get 100% Nick. I am sensitive to the environment and the occasion, but I will always communicate in a way that remains true to myself and a genuine version of who I am.

Once you become comfortable with your authentic self, communicating becomes so much simpler.

To test your authentic self and discover exactly who you are, I suggest you have a go at my 'Authenticity T-shirt' exercise.

The Authenticity T-Shirt

Take an A4 piece of paper and draw/print a basic, plain T-shirt outline.

On this shirt, I would like you to summarise yourself with a few words, or a picture if you wish, so that if you were walking down the street wearing your authenticity T-shirt and you came across someone you knew, they would be able to recognise you by your shirt alone. Summarise the very essence of who you are and distil this into a few simple words. Don't be tempted to create a separate shirt for work life and home life; this goes beyond that. A few words that get to the very heart of who you are, how you see yourself, and how you would like to be seen by others.

Take as long as you wish for this. Some people I work with are, boom, T-shirt sorted, ready to be worn with pride. Others really struggle. They have lengthy internal debates and still struggle to put who they truly are into words.

My T-shirt says:

Quirky, Fun, Optimistic, and Solid

One of my close relative's shirt (by his own admission) says:

Miserable Bastard

I would like to think this will change over time, but that's not up to me.

I've seen creative and personal versions of shirts and some simply with a question mark in the centre. In this case, one size does not fit all. Whatever you write on your shirt is entirely up to you. The only rule is it has to be you, your version of you.

At a workshop recently, I had a husband and wife sitting on the same table. When they looked at each other's shirts, neither of them agreed with how they had summed themselves up. It was extremely interesting and quite explosive. Fascinating to observe as they explored the reasoning behind their wording.

I have also had individuals take spare T-shirt sheets away to give to their partners. It's a medium that can open quite a dialogue and can be used for a host of discovery and communication reasons.

An additional level to this exercise, if used within teams, is to pass your shirt to your colleagues so they can add words to the back. The idea here is to discover aspects of ourselves that we are unaware of but are obvious to our workmates. Sometimes being made aware of these blind spots is enlightening.

The point of the exercise is that the words you choose to sum yourself up have massive implications on how you come across to others. These days I am always aiming to be totally authentic wherever I am. That wasn't always the case.

There was a time when there were two versions of me. A work and a home persona. I find this a lot, and huge numbers of people still live these two lives.

What I found was that as workload and pressure increased, the work version of me began to dominate, and the home version began to fade. Somewhere along the way, I lost the balance between the two Nicks. Work Nick began to encroach on my home life with disastrous consequences.

Those of you with two (plus) versions of your 'authentic' self, beware. As the pressures related to work increase, you may struggle to distinguish between your alternate versions. You may find yourself becoming someone you hardly recognise.

The best idea is to live as your true, authentic self. Be you. The words on your T-shirt are there for a reason. Live by them. In meetings, down the pub, at home, during hobbies, at lunch with your parents, in your kid's school, on holiday, and during the toughest of times.

Dare to be you, and the zombies will be petrified.

It's not easy. Ironically, it feels quite normal to put on airs and graces sometimes.

One of our family jokes is based on my mum's telephone voice; she quite often becomes the queen when communicating with strangers. We giggle about it, but it's natural. Just make sure you don't lose sight of the *you* in the communication.

I'm not saying that your authentic self will not develop and evolve over time. Similarly, if there is something on your T-shirt you aren't happy with, it is within your power to change it. We all have choices after all.

What I can promise you is that when you are truly comfortable in your authentic skin, your communication will come from the very heart of who you are. This can be so powerful. There is something wonderful and authoritative about using your true voice, straight from your authentic self. Those of you who have found your voice will already be aware of how influential you can be. Those of you still exploring what authenticity looks and feels like, it is so worth persevering.

I know. It's life-changing.

Working an Exhibition

"...and we'll see what happens
when we say Yes while this rigor
mortis world screams No."
— Isaac Marion, *Warm Bodies*

Trade shows or exhibitions are zombie-frenzy environments with the horde shuffling by your booth in quick succession. Your company has paid big money to be visible at the show, and the competition is all around you. The visitors have signed up to tour the floor and can expect to be targeted numerous times at every booth. It is not an ideal environment for friendly chats, although the networking opportunities are huge as most of your peers are likely to be in the hall.

Strangers walk by pretending to be on their phones, head down, and avoiding eye contact (typical zombie behaviour). Exhibitors are working hard to interrupt, attract, and draw the attention of every passer-by. It reminds me of a scene from an American department store, deep in the perfume/after-shave section — 'trade show for men', anyone?

It's not the most genuine of environments, and many organisations will have a gimmick or two to assist with attracting the eye towards their stand. When I work a trade show for a client, I enjoy the challenge of communicating in an exciting and congested space.

What I do is interrupt the traditional pattern of the bystander in a way they don't expect. With a big smile, I ask if they are having fun, if they have seen anything amazing, and I'm genuinely interested in their reply. The body language and micro-expressions tell me a great deal as to how this comment lands and what my next move is. If there is a hint of a smile, I turn my enthusiasm up a little and suggest what I consider to be the most fun aspect of the show (this could be a serious or a cheeky response depending on the interaction), and I work hard to encourage a conversation about anything that isn't related to the product on my stand. This way we are more likely to connect without the sales bias they have received throughout the day.

If they have been bombarded by the 'trade show for men' approach, (and there's a very good chance they have) an alternative approach is like a breath of fresh air.

I tend to ask a lot of questions to explore how they are motivated, how their day has been, and what interests them at the show. All of my responses can be made to measure based on the information gathered. If they are likely to benefit from our products and service, I will introduce these when appropriate.

People generally like to talk about themselves. If your focus is on the other person, their day, their likes/dislikes, then the conversation can progress without having to overcome burdensome hurdles.

Just like with the formal and traditional networking environment, I will exit out of the conversation when required using the past tense. A pleasant interaction is one thing, but you are there to work your butt off, so stay focused, and don't get drawn into the 'life-story' dialogue that some visitors will be overly-keen to divulge.

Compliment Day

"It is a great mistake for men to give up
paying compliments, for when they give
up saying what is charming, they give
up thinking what is charming."
— Oscar Wilde

Here's an exercise for you that may open some doors and may get you a few strange looks, which is always interesting. It's easy to do; we have the ability and power to make it happen whenever we desire. You may surprise yourself (you will definitely surprise others), and you may have an amazing adventure.

Have the courage to embark on a 'compliment day' in which you aim to deliver a compliment to as many people as you can during your travels. Start with one and work your way up to ten in a day. Once in the swing, there will be no stopping you. It is simple to do, but it takes a little nerve. Simply observe and compliment.

An easy place to begin is to compliment what people are wearing, how their hair looks, their nails, their bag, the book they're reading, all the external things that are readily on show. A more difficult, but powerful step is to dig a little deeper and compliment someone on how they carry themselves, their stance, their opinions, manners, focus, the more internal aspects of someone, who at this point is still a stranger.

The key to this exercise is that you are looking for nothing in return. Just deliver a compliment and be ready to continue with your day. The zombies will not be ready for this. The virus has mostly removed our nerve to say something that is out of the ordinary. If your observation begins a conversation, then great news. See where it goes and use the 'communicating with strangers' strategies covered so far to explore.

What a way to practise your new skills. You'll be adding value to a stranger's day, doing something lovely with no expectation of something in return, and you will be honing your communication expertise.

Imagine if we all did this on a regular basis. How would the world feel about itself? How many zombies would we wake from their reverie?

I was travelling across country recently, and as it was a lengthy drive, I stopped off for a latte to rest my aching limbs and refuel my senses. In the café, I came across a couple not typically dressed for the road. He was wearing a striking and almost outrageous purple shirt, and she a pair of purple killer heels. I was interested. I complimented them both. I admired the gentleman's shirt and told him how awesome it looked and told his companion I had not seen many shoes that could match her pair. They were dumbstruck. They were not expecting that. Who is?

It turned out they were on their way back from a funeral and had made clothing choices to be dazzling, striking, and to lift the normally sullen atmosphere that accompanies a funeral service. All of the guests had been encouraged to dress in a similar fashion.

We had a brief conversation, and I was on my way. They were taken aback and thrilled that I had mentioned their choices, and the world looked a tiny bit brighter because of it.

Simple, but courageous.

Admittedly, some people are going to think you're a bit weird; that's how sad the world has become in these Armageddon days. Don't let the occasional unpleasant reaction put you off. It takes real courage to slay zombies, so take bold steps and be sincere.

A simple compliment could reveal and unlock doors you never would have guessed existed. Strangers could become acquaintances. This could be the start of an incredible relationship. You may uncover common interests. Business may result.

Be courageous. Tackling the virus is not for the faint-hearted. It takes nerve and a healthy dose of audacity. Be prepared to enter your new orbit and stretch yourself. Your observation skills, your ability to deal with the unknown, and the levels of adventure you experience will increase.

SECTION 3

Defeating the Virus and Communicating with Your Tribe

"I have always liked the monster within
idea. I like the zombies being us.
Zombies are the blue-collar monsters."
— George A Romero

Take a quick look at your inbox. Do you have in excess of 100 emails unread? Virtual post queued up, piled high, and sitting around like the forgotten conversations they almost were. You are not alone. We are drowning in them, and they are next to useless!

It is very rare for me to come across an organisation that doesn't list email as one of their main communication hurdles.

Many years ago, I worked for a major broadcasting organisation. The organisation was chaotic, constantly undergoing change, and poor at communicating with itself. I found it strange that a company so highly acclaimed at communicating and getting through to global audiences was diabolical when it came to communicating one office to another — things didn't add up.

I have since learned that this particular company is no exception. Office politics, egos, one-upmanship, and multiple layers of management are all barriers to fluid and effective communication, and we are struggling under an epidemic of noise.

In a world where you receive an email from your colleague two desks away, there is something broken. We have changed, and it is not in keeping with how we as humans have developed. The alarm bells should be ringing across the land. The Armageddon is raging.

While enveloped within this organisation, I realised my communication skills had reached a new low. My email reliance had matched those of the corporation, and I was as ineffective as everyone else.

I knew it was out of hand when yet another email popped into my inbox alerting me to the fact that my allocated space on the email server was full, and I should arrange with my line manager a charge code so we could buy more space. Now I'm not an IT expert, but as a solution to a problem of inefficiency with emails, additional space for even more emails is surely not ideal. It's like the credit card companies giving you additional credit when you cannot curtail your spending habits — it is feeding a problem rather than providing a solution, and it's a problem that cannot end happily.

I had an alternative solution, however.

I deleted my inbox.

Cue gasps, the shaking of heads, and reactions of outrage. You can't do that, Nick. What were you thinking? Have you gone mad?

1000+ emails gone in a satisfying ping.

The fall-out from such a petulant and foolhardy reaction was, as it happens, nothing. My view was that if it's urgent, I will receive a chasing email, others will follow up, and I will soon be in the loop again. But there was not a single repercussion. Not one.

Now I'm not suggesting this is a viable solution to the communication virus that rages in your office, but it shouldn't give us nightmares either. When did we become so reliant on something that at one point was simply more convenient than a fax?

I am not alone in this rather empowering solution to email noise.

During a recent workshop, one of my delegates told me a story that should give us all hope.

This took place in Sweden, where there are strict rules around the appropriate use of email. One of their colleagues returned from holiday and was dismayed to find an inbox brimming with mail.

We've all been there. First day back from a wonderful break and your mailbox represents a massive pain in the rear end. Some of us fear this to the point that we dedicate some of our holiday time to keeping on top of the constant stream of noise generated by the zombie horde.

Some of us feel the urge to get up early on holiday so we don't interrupt the family time scheduled for normal waking hours. We're on holiday, and we can't let go!

My delegate's colleague was visibly disturbed by the weight of the pending inbox-clearing work ahead. This was picked up by their keen-eyed manager, who came across to explore the problem.

Her response? Seeing one of her team distressed and brought immediately out of that holiday positivity by the email burden, she leant across his desk, highlighted all his emails, and hit delete.

Yeah! That's powerful and invigorating leadership.

Her view was that after a holiday, you should feel energised, positive, and raring to go. She took ownership of the very thing that was instantly preventing this from being the case.

I have since discovered others that regularly delete emails once they are a month old, even if they have not been dealt with, and there are courageous organisations, leading the way, who have banned the use of emails for internal communication. The world is changing slowly, but the virus spreads at speed.

My point here is that we have moved towards a series of communication methods that are on the one hand, simple and time-saving, but on the other, mostly ineffective. Emails, in particular, are a victim of their own success, and in 90% of cases are not as effective as a phone call or even a hand-written letter! My generation (I'm 48 at the time of writing this) is the email generation. We saw the start (1993-ish), and I would like to think we will also see the end of email as we currently know it. Don't tell anyone, but I think we killed email by overuse, and it is not long for this world. RIP email. Good riddance. We need to refashion it to be something formal for legal and binding information and for document transfer. As a communication format, it sucks!

Perhaps we should mention this to those who are responsible for sending more than 250 billion emails every day!

If we want to achieve more, we need to be much smarter in the way we communicate. We need to converse with more passion, have greater impact in the office, and affect others at a much deeper level than we currently do.

We need to change, we have to, and we can.

Modern communication surrounds us like an ocean. We're drowning, and we only have ourselves to blame. We can choose another way. Why swim for our lives when we can learn to surf, rise up, and ride the waves of zombie noise?

Consider your last piece of communication. Have a think about the last time you attempted to send a message, have a conversation, hold a meeting, or present to an audience. How much other 'noise' was your audience experiencing at the time? How distracting were the crashing waves of digital commotion? I observe audiences in all communication environments that are preoccupied and supposedly multi-tasking on their personal devices. Does this confused picture make a difference to how you decide to share your message?

Think for a moment about the last time you were struck with a piece of communication that actually got through, landed, made an impact, and enabled change to occur. What did that feel like? How did it look, and what effect did it have on you and your universe?

I was knocked off my feet by a simple but life-changing message recently, and it had an incredible impact on me, my work, and my future. Sounds amazing, huh? It was only fifteen words, fifty-three letters in total.

The message was not delivered by a judge, nor a man of the cloth. It didn't come to me in a dream or via email. It was a simple conversation with my beautiful fiancée who has a unique view of the world, and she lent me her powerful insight.

"You don't have to be a perfectionist; you just have to get on with it."

Simple, huh? It's not rocket science, but it got through. It was perfectly timed and delivered with love, and it changed everything.

I used to be a perfectionist, used to strive for that unreachable, flawless solution that actually doesn't exist. I'm not saying there is anything wrong with striving for the best you can do — in fact, I heartily encourage it — but seeking perfection was holding me back.

I see the chasing of this *dream* holding many others back too.

There were certain things I would delay and procrastinate over before attempting because, in my mind, everything had to be perfect. In reality, the fun is in the doing, so anything holding you back needs to be questioned.

I can't make things perfect, but I can happily give a task my all, and it turns out I am happy with outstanding.

Sometimes, the most powerful communication can be the simplest message. It just needs to be delivered the right way. This simple truth is so often lost in the viral Armageddon.

Whatever your communication needs and motivations, the solutions are the same: powerful and impactful strategies, a healthy dose of courage, and some formidable attitudes for getting through. Whether you need to communicate with a new audience, apply a fresh and dramatic sense to your message, or are overwhelmed by noise and need to ensure your messages still land, it's time for courageous change.

There is a dated idiom that refers to someone who says big things but never acts on them — *'All mouth and no trousers'*. We are surrounded by examples of this within our many, varied tribes. I use the word *tribes* to mean teams at work, you and your colleagues, or groups who work or play together.

Within the office, you are witness to plenty of communication, and sadly this is mostly noise. There is a mass of information flying around every office, and far too little of it is focused on *getting stuff done*.

When was the last time you received an email and knew instantly what was required of you and why it was important? At its most basic, this is what email is for, surely? The reality is that, as with most office-based communication, email has become a vehicle for sharing information, not one for making things happen.

It doesn't help that we receive far too many emails every day. Stop adding to this nonsense!

Imagine if every time you communicated, action resulted. Team members acted on your commands and requests, friends took on board advice you offered, and bosses actually stopped, listened, and valued your input. Oh, what a marvellous world that would be.

Why on earth is it not the case? It's because we are watering down our communication to fill the ocean of noise that drowns the corporate and social worlds we swim in. We are simply adding to the zombie soup, lazily allowing the virus to spread and infect at every level.

There is a reason you are most productive the day before you embark on a holiday. You are focused on getting stuff done. You are in the zone because at some point there will be a plane taking off, and you need to be on it! I bet your emails are a damn sight shorter on that day.

This focus and your resulting application is brought on by urgency but is rarely maintained once we arrive home from two weeks sunning ourselves in some far away land.

Here comes another choice.

You decide how impactful and outcome-focused you want your communication to be. When you are questioned (by the zombies) for being direct, you'll know you are making superb progress.

We are surrounded by time management advice and labour-saving devices, but we are still starving for the time we need to live a contented, adventurous, and fun-filled life. Most of us are working more hours (in the office and at home), have more demands on our time than ever before, and are struggling to maintain our relationships, our health, and our sense of humour.

It's not surprising that the virus is spreading with such speed. We are weakened, and to succeed in this Armageddon takes effort.

There is a way out of this, but you've got to get a grip and take back control. Swim against the tide and rise above the waves of the groaning horde.

When communicating with your tribe, your work colleagues, your social club, your friends, and your family, concentrate on the *why*. Why am I communicating? What am I looking to achieve? What is the best way to make this happen?

Consider your options. What gives you the best chance of success first time? It's rarely the type of emails we see on a daily basis. Communicate once, think about it, and make it count.

Consider a two-minute phone call, a one-line email, a text message, a LinkedIn update — what is most likely to get through and have the impact that will make a difference? What will resonate with your tribe and get through on a human level?

There is a reason that many of the most modern methods of communicating are in a much shorter form than the more 'traditional' corporate techniques. They are designed to achieve more in a shorter time and with fewer words. They appeal to an emerging generation (or two) who will not put up with lengthy, wordy nonsense. But beware the zombie tendency to ignore the human. Even the shortest message should have human characteristics.

These shorter forms of communicating lend themselves to collaborating through the magic of images too — these can often deliver impact much easier than our outmoded word-based communication. We can still embrace modern communication if we keep an eye on what motivates humans as opposed to zombies.

The world of communication is evolving, and it is likely to make us feel uncomfortable. Everything we learnt at school about spelling, grammar, punctuation, and writing formal letters has been overtaken by spellcheck and auto-correct or has been replaced by the new language of the web where symbols replace words and formality now means appropriate hashtags.

If you reminisce about the old days and long for a return to simpler times — stop it. There ain't no going back. Onwards and upwards we go into a new world with the understanding that our generation is the last to use paper dictionaries, thesauruses, maps, and notepads. We're also the last to write in full sentences punctuated with capital letters and full stops. RIP the old way. You can hang onto it, but your kids won't.

I must admit, this used to worry me. I was concerned that my kids wouldn't be able to transition into a *traditional* work environment because it was increasingly foreign from the world they were growing up in. I was troubled by their screen-based existence. I know of a number of parents that have taken this fear to interesting lengths and have rationed their children's screen time.

Recent reports refer to social media as junk food and encourage boundaries for kids to enable a healthy digital '5 a day'. There are a host of differing views as to what are healthy and unhealthy approaches to the digital domain. My concern is that very few of these approaches highlight the need to humanise the digital communication approach.

It took me a while to realise that our kids will be masters of the new world, and it is our time and the reign of our old-school communication that is limited. Our biggest challenge is how to maintain the human connection in this digital world.

I discussed this recently during a training session with a company who are captains of their industry but are steeped in 'old-school' thinking. During the conversation, the only delegate in the room under the age of twenty simply nodded and informed the group that she only uses email at work, never away from the office. This is reflected in data that suggest only 6% of teenagers use email daily[6] – they have moved on to communicating through more *efficient* social networks. Our group of older and *wiser* professionals were bemused and then rather pensive.

How many of you have learnt your way around Facebook so you can communicate with your *friends*, have discovered LinkedIn so you can attract a wider audience, and have explored Twitter to make an instant digital impact? How many kids have signed up to business writing courses in comparison? Not many, I bet.

For those of you holding back and refusing to give in to the new platforms for communication — try not to fear it. Approach it all with the *why* of your communication strategy and make use of the best methods for getting your stuff done quicker and with more impact.

The zombie virus is not spreading at an alarming rate because the technology is preventing us from communicating. Rather, too many of us are hiding behind the tech and lazily letting it do all the work. We are forgetting that to really get through, we need to be human and adjust how we use current and future technology to enhance the human impact of how we communicate.

---

6   Amanda Lenhart, Pew Research, 2012

The best communication technology will enable more human interaction, not replace it!

If you are using social media to put your point across, add some authentic emotion to your posts. Give your authentic self and worry less about maintaining a persona. If you are posting information online, let your audience know how it makes you feel, what it looks like to you, and how we could benefit from your perspective. If using digital communication to have a *conversation,* remove anything that doesn't sound like you. Imagine what the interaction would be like if you were face to face, and as much as is prudent, allow the content to reflect the human.

To truly get through to your audience, you need to communicate in a way that resonates and requires a more human interaction.

In a nutshell:

- Think *why* — what are you looking to achieve?
- Think *who* — ways of getting through to this particular audience.
- Think *how* — the medium that is most likely to work.
- Get it done. Stay human.

Motivating and Influence

"It is not the horse that draws the cart,
but the oats." — Proverb

A key ingredient to getting your stuff done and being successful with your outcomes is to effectively motivate your audience. It helps to put yourself in their shoes and see the world from their side of the table, but we can do even more than that to turbo-charge our impact and stay ahead of the horde.

What is it that your audience *want*? There is a tendency to concentrate on what we believe our audience *needs*, but this isn't the factor that will drive their activity — it's all about what they want.

I need a new guitar. My old one has been adopted by my son, and it has disappeared off to university. He made it sound better than I did, so I was happy to let it go. Now, however, I need a new one. I miss not being able to pick it up and spread a little music through the house. There are a number of tunes I would like to emulate, and it would be therapeutic to once again pluck at the strings.

Do I need one? Or do I want one?

I want one. The reasons above are me justifying this want into a need. They are sound (excuse the pun) reasons, but I don't actually *need* one.

Emotion is a very powerful motivator, more so than good old common sense. We may *need* a new car, and that need could be satisfied by any number of reasonable makes and models, but what we *want* is something 'sporty'. We'll happily justify this want to ourselves and others by a host of rational needs, but what we want will be the driver (there he goes again with another pun) to make many of us purchase the possibly less suitable sporty number.

Most of us work this way. We are motivated by our 'wants', and these are connected to our emotions and the feelings associated with who we are.

So this means that when communicating, we should carefully consider what our audience *wants*, not what they need or what we need/want for that matter.

We may need better security, but what we want is to feel safer. We need to eat a balanced diet and exercise regularly, but what we want is to be pain-free, energetic, and feel healthy. You may need to sell more widgets, but what you really want is to hit your target and earn that lovely bonus.

Think wants, not needs; think plants, not weeds.

Plant communication that has a positive impact, not *noise* that assaults and doesn't add value.

Zombies happily attack communication with need-based content. Lots and lots of stuff, bombarding the senses with information. Emails by the bucket-load, messages of no real value, constantly streaming in all directions, lacking the focus to actually get through.

If you are communicating with your boss, for example, consider what motivates them. What do they truly want? Let's imagine they want less stress and more profits, which sounds reasonable, then our contact with them should focus on the aspects that remove stress and increase return on investment. That is sure to get them really listening.

If you are communicating with your partner, consider what they truly want, and motivate them with messages that focus on this and combine your wants into this mix.

Blending your wants with the wants of others often takes a little work. For example, we may want our kids to keep their rooms tidy, but what they want is to be left alone and to make their space their own. If we simply communicate from our perspective, we're likely to be up against it.

"I've told you a thousand times to keep this pit tidy. I can't believe you can live like this. You're worse than an animal!"

Oh, the joy of parenthood.

If we balance the two wants (ours and theirs), we are far more likely to get through. Think human. In this case, our communication could centre on the idea of more independence (their wants) and a room that truly reflects their personality (ideally our wants). This would mean we would talk about crafting a space that suits who they are with a compromise of putting their dirty washing in the laundry basket and removing any used crockery and rubbish as this is not a true reflection of their character.

It's a blend, but it ultimately stems from their 'wants'.

Get through with a flexible approach but maintain your authenticity. Long term this will keep the virus at bay because of your ability to explore the human 'wants' that will promote dynamic action.

When you have an opportunity to influence your audience, consider what the 'wants' are, and work creatively to cater to both sides of this interesting dynamic.

The more influential you become, the more the zombies will fear your machete.

One-to-One — Conversations Worth Having

> "I learned that a long walk and
> calm conversation are an incredible
> combination if you want to build a
> bridge." — Seth Godin

The most common human communication process in the office and beyond is a one-to-one discussion. Do this well, with power and focus, and you can achieve incredible success. As the virus spreads, this simple and effective method of getting through is fading into the electronic background.

How often do you come away from a conversation at work or beyond and wonder what the point was? Unless you are passing the time, catching up, or simply conversing as part of your daily entertainment, then there is power in a conversation worth having. These are the conversations that get things done, that enable progress, and develop ideas.

If you're sharing information to improve a set of circumstances, start by putting yourself in the other person's shoes. What does the situation look like from their perspective, how does the world look to them? If you are conversing with a zombie, take your time and focus. Their attention will soon be drifting. Listen actively, concentrate on what is and is not being said. Explore the best win-win solutions that you can see at this point, try a few options, select alternatives. Agree on a next step and set about doing things differently. Check in as regularly as you need to make sure the progress continues, and be prepared to change direction if the first path is not serving you both.

All sound a bit too easy? Is this possible? Do these strategies actually work? Can *we* use them?

The next time you're involved in an important conversation, one which is designed to progress an idea or improve a situation, use the following checklist to see how effective it has and continues to be:

- Do I empathise — can I see the world through their eyes?
- Do we both understand the other's point of view? Do we have rapport?
- Have we discussed a solution that suits us both?
- Do we know what happens next and what that looks like?

The one-to-one dialogue is a little like your putting game at golf; it is rarely practised and seldom taught as a key skill. We are more likely to spend time at the driving range and let loose with the big guns, knocking a bucket of balls into the ether. This is the equivalent of preparing yourself for those big event communication opportunities, like your formal presentations. Your one-to-ones are far more prevalent though. You may drive off a number of times, but you will be putting at least twice as much. Do it poorly, and it will destroy your scorecard.

So what does a powerful discussion look like?

- Goal — machete-like clarity
- Journey — navigating the horde
- Diversions — human vs zombie
- Arrival — a little less virus

Goal

Know where you are going or you may end up going nowhere. If you know what you are looking to accomplish from your one-to-one discussion, you're far more likely to achieve a positive outcome. Be clear about your goal. What does it look like? How does it feel? Consider the position of the other participant and listen actively.

It's a pain in the butt and really frustrating once you realise you're both looking for different outcomes from your discussion and haven't a clue how to progress at least half of the conversation.

So about this bonus payment I am due?

Oh, I thought you were here to talk about the sponsored walk?

Err, no. We were always going to talk about my bonus. Remember my email entitled, 'Making progress towards increased success'?

Oh, you were talking about financial steps? I thought…

If you are simply chatting to pass the time, catch up, and enjoy the company of others, then these are your goals. Don't lose sight of them or you run the risk of being diverted into a conversation that you'd rather not be part of.

Clarity around your goals and the agenda of others will provide the focus you need to construct a conversation that produces results. Even if the exchange is spontaneous, if there is an objective, then the clearer you can see that, the more likely you are to head in the right direction.

Ask yourself what would be a really good outcome for you and for them. What is it that would make this conversation worthwhile? Maximise the interaction and make it so much more worthwhile than a zombie-style email exchange.

Journey

Have a plan and a route for achieving your goal, and be prepared to take a diversion or two along the way. Part of the adventure of communication is dealing with the unknown, the roadblocks that will need to be navigated and overcome to successfully reach your destination.

If you are observant and perceptive, then most of these roadblocks will be clearly signposted and will give you plenty of warning so you can reroute accordingly.

The office gossip, *oh have you heard who is likely to be heading out the door*, style of interruption does nothing but fuel the politics of Zombieland. It feels like we are part of the tribe, but we are promoting noise (juicy noise, but still, noise) and being adopted into the horde. Unless your conversation is for catching up on office gossip, then beware these distractions. Be ready to bring the discussion back on track to your journey plan.

Diversions

During a conversation, look for emotional leakage and body language signals (explored in detail in our section on *Reading the Signals)* to accompany the words being exchanged. This way you can get inside the head of the other person to check how the discussion is landing. If you observe something non-congruent (they are saying one thing but their body language is saying something else), this gives you an opportunity to divert, to slow down, and to check they are OK with the dialogue so far. Ask a few questions to check how the information is being received. Explore the good points and perhaps highlight any areas that are causing them concern. Many of the potential roadblocks and diversions can be avoided with this early warning system. Your zombie colleagues are hopeless at this. Their *dead* senses simply do not pick up on these essential signals.

If your communication has caused a quirk in the expected body language of the other party, then it makes sense to pause, ask a few pertinent questions, and let the other person speak. Listen with your ears and your eyes, and investigate further to see if you are facing a roadblock or some other idiosyncrasy.

Arrival

If you know what you are looking to achieve, you should recognise it once you have arrived. Also, be prepared for what happens next and what this means for both parties.

Take the successful arrival at your destination on board, and sow the seeds for the next step. This may simply be a mental note of future conversations and discussions, or it may be something formal, like planning the next one-to-one meeting.

We are entering conversations repeatedly throughout our day. If they are human, face to face, and one-to-one, then we have an opportunity to make things happen and leave the undead shuffling at their snail's pace. Sharpen your machete with these simple guidelines and make progress through the interactions worth having.

Listening — Through the Zombie Groans and Beyond

> "There is a difference between
> listening and waiting for your turn to
> speak." — Simon Sinek

If we remove the formality of this one-to-one approach, you can turn this method to any type of dialogue in which you are looking to make some progress. Chats with your family, sociable conversations with your colleagues, or discussions with friends can all benefit from some focus, direction, and a proactive strategy.

On the top of your list, when communicating informally, should be to listen. Work hard to be present and in the moment (this may mean turning off the TV), and listen with your ears and your eyes. Don't miss an opportunity to pick up some extra detail from the body language.

Even though we can't be very effective multitaskers, if we listen with as much application as we can muster, it's amazing what we can absorb. The toughest part of this process is giving ourselves permission to stop, focus, and truly listen. Be proactive with your listening. Soak everything up so you are fully equipped to respond when the time is right.

The virus assaults the senses of our zombie friends until their perception is wafer thin or possibly non-existent.

I was on the phone some time ago with a colleague and friend. We were catching up and talking about business. As the conversation turned to how well business was going, the conversation went like this:

So, how are things? Business good?

No, not really, mate. Things are really quiet.

Oh, good, good. Glad to hear that.

In other words, he was not listening and didn't give a hoot about my response. It was a disappointing exchange and shone a light on the zombie virus working its way into his communication.

The success of our relationships and the degree to which we enjoy the company of others has a great deal to do with how we communicate our needs and wants and how we respond to the wishes and desires of others. If we listen to what our friends, family, and colleagues are *really* saying and respond in a productive and empathetic way, we will have far more win-win interactions.

We can't please everyone, and I don't believe we should even try, but we can have magical relationships based on understanding, fairness, and growth, especially with those we care for.

My younger self (and my not-so-younger self) was focused on pleasing as many people as possible, and this had a detrimental effect on my connections. If you are in a win-lose relationship of any kind, don't expect this to be fruitful or long-lasting. Even if you are the 'losing' party and the other half of the relationship is reaping all the benefits, this cannot go on indefinitely. At some point, the demands will grow beyond your capabilities, or the shine will fade from your delivery, and why wouldn't it if you're not reaping any of the rewards?

The only long-term strategy for relationship building is one in which both parties win. Communicating with integrity, passion, and purpose, and listening like a pro are the best weapons at your disposal to bring you both success.

Zombie Home

"A house is not a home unless it
contains food and fire for the mind as
well as the body." — Benjamin Franklin

One of the saddest aspects of the modern Armageddon is the crumbling of quality conversations at home. Think for a moment and give your interactions at home a score between 1 and 10.

1 means there has been merely a series of grunts and acknowledgements, and 10 means you could star in a Hollywood musical as you are totally in tune!

How do you score?

Typically, your day could look like this:

Interaction	Score	What is Really Going On
Partner (before work)	4	Need coffee, in a rush, lots to do.
Partner (after work)	5	A few moans and groans about work and our daily exploits.
Partner (evening)	3	TV, smartphone, and other distractions.
Kids (before work)	1	We're all in the land of the zombie.

Kids (after work)	2	Minimal interaction. They don't want to hear from us.
Kids (evening)	2	They're in their room, distractions fired up to the hilt.

If you're scoring much higher than this, congratulations, you are bucking the trend and keeping the virus at bay. Good work. If, however, the above scores are a reasonable reflection of your day (for some, they may be even worse), then you are among the majority. We are sliding down the zombie path and allowing the most important stuff to slip away.

We are finding time to check our emails, no problem. We spend quality time on Facebook without a worry. We dip into Twitter, Snapchat, WhatsApp, and Instagram, but we're struggling to find the time to interact with those we care for most. I regularly hear from people who complain that they and their partner don't talk any more. Evenings are spent on devices, shielded from real interaction, distracted by the zombie noise.

A text message can interrupt even the most intimate conversations.

"I know you're telling me that you love me, but that was my phone buzzing. Let me just check who needs me."

Can we really spend more than eight hours interacting with our digital devices every day? When are we finding time to do anything else? Or are we?

We all have smartphones and hardly ten minutes can go by without us craving a fiddle with our devices. We check our phones 150 times a day, and it is changing what it means to be human.

One of my delegates recounted a recent trip she had made to her local pub. It was a Saturday, and the venue had some music playing. The atmosphere was jovial, the drinks flowed, and the evening was in full swing. There was a young couple at a nearby table, and both were hooked on their digital devices. The DJ made an announcement, and the music stopped. The young lad left his phone alone and bent down on one knee. This was the moment. Everything stopped, and the pub watched as he asked his girl to be his wife. She said yes, and there was much joy, and then they were back on their phones as though nothing had changed.

This story was told to me in all seriousness. It's not made up. It actually happened and is not that unusual in the land of the zombie. When you reach for your phone to update your relationship status before reaching for your partner's hand, you know the virus has you. If you hunger to feed your noise to the world more than you crave a meaningful conversation, you know you are part of the horde. This is the way the world is heading.

We are drowning in this ocean of noise, and the volume and intensity continues to increase. What we are all experiencing is the incessant noise of the zombie horde, continually advancing. The unprepared will be consumed by their meaningless clamour.

Consider your scores. How do you feel about them? Do they need to improve? What are you going to do to improve them? Will you dare to fight the virus and wield your machete?

The first steps do not need to be outrageous. Let's not get overly obsessed and unplug the WiFi, but let's do something to redress the balance. Have an hour of human. No devices, no noise, just you and those you care about. Catch up, listen, giggle, and share stories.

See how it feels. Open the door to an alternative to the virus-laden distractions which are dumbing down our emotions and our ability to care. Be brave and be different. Keep those machetes sharp.

Tough Stuff

"No one loves the messenger
who brings bad news."
— Sophocles, *Antigone*

More often than not, the tough stuff requires true human connection. If you've ever been on the receiving end of difficult news delivered badly with no compassion and lacking an ounce of empathy, you will know it leaves you shaken, angry, and looking for someone to blame.

If it is delivered with compassion and understanding, your response is likely to be very different.

When I received challenging news in my younger days, fortunately, it was communicated by a human and not a zombie. We all filed into the presentation hall, the atmosphere a blend of excitement and trepidation. There was a buzz that hinted at a series of important messages to come. We took our seats and waited patiently, the bright neon lights overhead clashing with the brightly coloured plastic seating.

Senior management was in attendance. The CEO stood up to address the teams.

"Thank you all for coming. I know you are all eager to know the decisions that the board have come to. We have decided to make the entire sales and marketing teams redundant."

This news could not be delivered within a win-win framework. Ironically, those who were let go at that time will probably look back and thank their lucky stars they escaped when they did.

The news of the impending mass redundancies was delivered to the entire organisation in an open style. The board were insistent that the information would be communicated to the entire group at the same time. This minimised the chance of third-party-generated rumour and lessened the chance of the management team being attacked by *passionate* individuals!

Tough stuff to hear and then have to deal with, but the news was received in an open and authentic way. Questions were answered for as long as the audience wanted the details explained. As far as bad news goes, it could have been much worse.

There are times when a win-win will not be your top priority. When your interaction has a specific purpose, and may not be well received by the other party, the win-win ideal may be beyond your reach. I suggest you keep the best outcome (for both parties) in mind, but reality may dictate that this is more of a luxury than a necessity. More and more of the zombie communication I witness is delivered with no thought about the receiver whatsoever. We can do better.

If you are reprimanding a colleague, for example, your communication may well be about highlighting an issue and working towards a suitable outcome. This may not be welcome by the other party but still, the discussion has to happen. Similarly, passing on bad news may not produce a positive outcome but can still be done using compassion, empathy, and understanding.

Communicating bad news or information that is not likely to be well received requires a change in body language and tone. Go for softer body language: open arms, palms-up hand gestures, and head tilts to maximise the empathy in your delivery. If you are reprimanding someone, use your powerful and closed non-verbal communication: straight head, minimal eye contact, palm down, and much shorter, quicker gestures.

Even if you are communicating unwelcome news, you can still ensure your messages are delivered with power. Your presence, an ethical leadership approach, and your authenticity should allow you to come across with authority.

Powerful communication is focused, the points are clear, what we want and what we want from others is evident, there should be no need to labour the issue. Add a solid stance: feet shoulder-width apart, hips square, maintain steady eye contact — don't zombie stare — and pause regularly to allow your *magic* to sink in. Use authoritative gestures such as 'palm down pointing' (hand horizontal with the floor, index finger extended, and thumb exposed — a bit like a child-like gun shape but on its side) to smooth out the issues and 'chopping' (one palm facing upwards, as though you were balancing a plate in front of you, and the other hand acting as a karate-chop style knife in a chopping motion) to *cut* through the potential hurdles.

Work hard to become an influencer, share your outstanding ideas, and deliver your messages in a controlled and measured way.

Breaking Down Barriers

Those of you who enjoy a challenge, (I certainly do) have a go at breaking down a few barricades. Often, hostile communication barriers are put up by others in a vain attempt to either hide from reality or to try and make their point stand out. Neither of these reasons are strong enough for you to let them get away with their obstacles.

Break those bad boys down!

Get stuck into a political discussion. Take an opposing view to the company gossip. Approach a debate from an alternative direction and see how it feels.

Some people are extremely opinionated. It's rare, however, to find an opinionated person whose opinions are worth listening to.

Use a commanding blend of listening, empathetic mirroring, and tactical questioning to get inside their head and explore their opinions and tackle them from within.

A useful first response when faced with a forceful opinion is to smile; it unbalances the other party and creates a glimmer of uncertainty. You may be smiling because you know better, you agree, you find it amusing or entertaining. It allows you space to breathe, to listen, and observe.

This art of active listening and careful observation is being lost in the waves of the zombie advance. In most parts of the world, we don't seem to take the time to stop any more.

It's useful to know where the opinion is really coming from, and what's provoking the hostility. You may want to dig a little deeper. To do this you will need to ask pertinent questions: the 'what' and the 'why'.

What is it that's driving that series of ideas?
What are you basing that theory on?
What else could you use to explain that?
Why do you feel that is the best conclusion from these thoughts?

Why does that have to be the only answer?
Why don't we step back and take a broader view?

Throw in the speculative 'what if' question to put an alternative string of thought into the mix.

What if there was another way?
What if we had to change how we make that happen?
What if you woke up tomorrow and the world looked different?

Be polite, see things from their point of view if humanly possible, and respond with authenticity and interest in a calm and measured way. They may not like it, but they may not like a lot of things. Remember, your opinion matters just as much as theirs.

Don't waste too much of your valuable time with the opinionated buffoon, the zombie's biggest fan, but be interested in the fine line between passion, exuberance, and hostility. It's often valuable to explore and look for common ground.

At one of my recent workshops, I was challenged by a delegate who really didn't want to be in the room. This is a typical hurdle for whoever is delivering a course when attendance is compulsory. When faced with a reluctant visitor, you want to explore the opportunities and discover the potential disruptions that may result. Are they a zombie or are they human?

Answer these questions if you can:

Can I work with this individual?

Will they make it difficult or uncomfortable for the rest of the group?

Could I turn their reticence to my advantage?

Are we talking about slaying or curing the virus?

As long as they aren't going to be a pain in the rear end for you and everyone else, there is a potential adventure to be had. When appropriate, I suggest as early as possible to investigate their position and why they are not embracing the opportunity to learn, collaborate, and develop. Listen well and watch the body language. Watch for body signals that are not in keeping with the words they are using — discover their 'tells', those unconscious movements or twitches that illustrate their discomfort.

Based on your observation and proactive listening, you should have an idea as to their underlying issues.

Use the 'what if' style of questions to open their mind and find some common ground while highlighting the value you can bring.

In my case, the delegate was cruising into retirement and was looking forward to escaping all things corporate. His feeling was that my course was another aspect of the world he was soon to be leaving far behind him. I shared his pending retirement excitement and dug a little deeper to see what he had planned once the corporate landscape was in his rear-view mirror. It didn't take long to discover that there were a host of things he was planning that my course would resonate with. As an added incentive to be 100% present, I asked for his help and support with those who were much newer into the organisation and the industry — his experience, after all, would be enlightening.

He participated fully and loved the course and was a real asset in the room. Slaying potential zombies before they infect all those around them is definitely worth a few minutes of exploratory communication.

Surfing Above the Horde

"Who you are tomorrow begins with
what you do today." — Tim Fargo

For me, communication has a few key attributes: to get things done, to entertain, and to assist in the journey to successful outcomes. Too often I come across interactions that are generating great amounts of output but very little progress. We are sinking beneath the ever-rising waters of the communication ocean, and if you want to succeed, you will need to either swim better than everyone else, or surf above the waves of the tempestuous horde. Swimming in the turbulent waters is exhausting, so jump on board. Surf's up!

Have you ever sent a series of emails with the best intentions in the world, but for several reasons they didn't have the desired effect? Ever been to a meeting where plenty was said and even agreed but very little transpired? Ever had a really interesting conversation that was well received by all parties but didn't go anywhere? If you answered, "*yes indeed, Nick*" to any or all of these, then you know what swimming in the stormy and crowded communication waters is like — it's rubbish!

What is it you were looking for from these interactions? You send your email, the recipient opens it, reads it, does what you suggest, and things get better. Your meeting is productive, your team go away energised, make the action points a reality, and things get better. Your conversation is enlightening, both you and the other parties improve on their approach to the subject at hand, and things get better.

Things get better!

If that isn't what happens every time you communicate, then you can do better.

We rapidly come back to focus and choices. Try a revolutionary and courageous approach. Take half the time, and use half the words, but use your time wisely, and choose your words with care and with the outcome in mind.

Turbo Emails — Machete the Go-To Office Tool

If you intend to send any emails (I'm not asking you to give it up, just suggesting some strategies to help), you have to begin with the 'why'.

Why are you sending this message to those particular people, and what exactly are you looking to achieve?

Let's assume you have received a hundred emails, and you have to deal with them effectively. A typical approach would look like the following:

- Scroll through the list of emails and delete any that are not relevant (marketing materials, Canadian pharmacies, unclaimed inheritances, Facebook updates). This should rid you of 90% of your intake, for now.
- Read the titles/sender of the remainder and decide which ones should be opened first. This could range from internal office requests, customer-focused enquiries, direct orders, or invites to social

events.

- Open the ones you are expecting or that sound interesting.
- Follow up (probably with an email response) those you were expecting. Be distracted by those that *sounded* interesting.
- Leave the ones that sound important enough to read at some point, knowing full well that once they drop off your first page of mail, they are likely to be forgotten.

Sound familiar?

It is typical and extremely poor communication. Email is broken. In the land of the zombies, email will eventually suck all the human from your interactions. If the list above is typical behaviour and you recognise it, just consider for a moment that your emails are also given this treatment by your recipients. How much of your electronic communication is getting through?

Not a lot!

Email is a master at the perception of 'being heard' with minimal amount of 'getting through'. What would happen if we just stopped? No more emails, ever. Would the world grind to a halt? Probably not. So why are we so reliant on this method of communication? We have been absorbed by its *convenient* embrace, and we are allowing it far too much importance. How did that happen? Surely we are not that important that we need to be at our desks sending and responding to emails all day long as though the universe depends on us?

Email: time saver, my arse!

So if you're still sending emails (we all are), then let's make them as effective as they can be. Let's take our machetes to them so they make it into the 1% that actually get read and actioned.

Firstly, consider if email is the best way to communicate your message. Don't default to it because it is easy, quick, and *effective*; it is not as impactful as you may think.

If email is the best option, consider what you are looking to achieve. This is hopefully a double-edged answer as we should be achieving something for ourselves (requesting details of hours worked over a set period for example) and something for the recipient (so we can ensure they are being paid the correct amount). When you are clear on your goals for this particular email, you are in a position to actually communicate in a way that produces results.

Make sure you don't lose the plot! Stick to the plan. Don't drift into other areas and begin a lengthy conversation about other topics. Stay human though. Add a little you, a personal touch, and something specific for your recipient. A lengthy conversation is much better face to face or over the phone, so don't overdo it.

Allow yourself a reasonable *human* greeting, and then get into the meat of your correspondence. Make your request and give the reason *why* this is important *for them*. You can even lead with the reasons why they will benefit from your request to motivate them to take action.

Let them know how they should respond to your request, make it as easy as possible for them to reply, and also (if appropriate, and it usually is) give them a timescale for the response.

Excellent. Sign off in a suitable way. Job done — almost.

We need to make sure they open your email in the first place, so give it a title that speaks to *them*. Wear their shoes for a moment and ask yourself what it is that would motivate them to open the email as a priority. Don't allow your message to become one of those slipping off page one. Zombies love an inbox crammed with noise. Don't add to their drooling mess.

More often than not, what motivates your audience is something about *them*, something beneficial or of value *to them*. Don't think about what you want at this stage, focus on their needs and ask yourself, 'if it was me, would I open this email first?'

The art of getting through requires alternative, courageous, and different approaches, and your email titles are one of the many places that this is absolutely essential.

Would you open an email that was titled '*FYI*'? Not likely. How about '*Update from Smith & Co*'? Nope, straight onto the delete list. What about '*Your Essential Guide to…*'? Once again, binned and not even close to being opened.

How about '*Nick, here are your travel documents*', '*Are you free on Friday to join us in London*', '*I saw you in town but didn't get a chance to say hi*', '*Our Sales Figures — summary for the last six months*'? These are far more likely to be opened as they speak directly to me.

Machete Emails — Are Your Emails This Sharp?

- Hi (stay human)
- Why
- What
- When
- Awesome Title

- Bye

Take a look at your recent emails and give them the **Hi WWW AB** machete test to see if they are fit to slice through the noise.

If they pass the test, you are well on your way to being more productive, more influential, and it should free up a mass of 'desk' time. Take that, horde!

If your communication is based on 'getting things done', you will be ahead of the game, ahead of the crowd, and potentially ahead of the competition. Clang your machete against your desk and enjoy the satisfying ring of virus-battling success.

The next time you send an email, cut it in half. Just say the essential stuff to ensure your outcome is front and centre of the recipient's attention. No fluff, just juice!

After all, if you are looking for a conversation, pick up the phone. Use your emails as a method of getting stuff done, not as a poor replacement for a chat.

Try it now.

Stop reading for a moment and dive into your inbox. Check the last email you sent and consider how you could make it just as powerful and outcome-focused using only two or three lines of text. How much could you achieve if every email you sent for a whole week only contained two or three lines maximum? OK, don't panic, there are going to be a few that require one or two more lines but make these the exception to your new two-line rule.

Could you do this for a week? Try adding the following text to your email signature:

Your time is precious, so I am working hard to deliver

incredible focus to my emails. I am using the two-line rule — power through brevity.

Don't allow yourself to slack because your emails are shorter. Work really hard to make the two lines as detailed as they need to be. Focus, clarity, output.

Greeting:

Include something that speaks to them. Flex your humanity. Allow yourself to enjoy writing this email.

Line 1:

Include what it is you are looking for/want them to do/solution you're providing/answer to their request etc.

Line 2:

Let them know how you want them to respond/method of preferred communication/time frame/what your expectations are/what you will do with their response/information.

Don't forget to include a title that motivates them to open the email, and you are most of the way there.
For example:

Title: Keith, to ensure you achieve your bonus this month

Greet: Morning Keith, I hope your daughter's graduation was full of joy. I know how that feels.

Line 1: To make sure I can collate the bonus for November, I will need your sales figures for all of *X*, *Y*, and *Zs* you've sold. I'm really excited to crunch those numbers as I know it has been an outstanding month.

Line 2: If you can send these across to me on a spreadsheet by Friday, I can make sure the figures are collated in time for the bonus payment. You'll then just have to plan how you're going to spend the money.

You can make these more succinct if you wish. I like to add a reasonable amount of my personality in emails to increase the human and reduce any hints of the virus infecting my words.

Take a look at a few more of your most recent sent items. Would removing unnecessary text allow you to get things done more effectively? Are your emails overwhelming the world with noise?

Don't assume email should be your go-to option either. The two-line rule will soon lead to exasperation if you don't have the courage to consider alternative methods of getting through.

An email about bonuses could easily be a phone call and a brief conversation to motivate as well as achieve your sales figure request.

Your inbox is flooded — we know that. Even if you are efficient, you have too many folders to neatly store all of the noise, so some courageous choices and a different way may be your cure.

I know business owners who have changed their email address because their old email server is filled to capacity. How drastic is that? It would be like moving house because your mail has filled your hallway or working in your basement because your office is full of paperwork.

An alternative way, with a dash of human, will confuse the hell out of your zombies.

Focused Meetings

How about this alternative approach?

At your next meeting, adopt the following slaying techniques:

- Slash the time by half. Machete through the normal hour. Give yourself thirty minutes instead.
- Laser focus on the results. Know exactly what this meeting is designed to achieve.
- Invite only those who can make key decisions.
- Be prepared to cut to the chase immediately. No virus-style distractions.
- Not prepped to follow the agenda? Send someone who is less zombie and is prepared.
- Agree who is responsible for any next steps and put a time frame on the delivery.
- Detail outcomes in the *who, what, when* document.
- *Who* is responsible for the next step/outcome?
- *What* does the outcome look like? What can we expect to see?
- *When* will the outcome/task be complete?
- Stick to it. Hold everyone accountable — no excuses, no zombies.

Reflect on your last meeting. How much of the time was dedicated to the key decisions that needed to be made, and were you surrounded by the key decision makers? Did you stick to the agenda and stay on message? If the answer is anything but 'absolutely', you can cut some time from the gathering.

This is a strategy that is easier to adopt if it's forced upon you. Those meetings that are shorter due to external reasons are likely to be far more focused than the weekly catch-up hour that only achieves ten minutes of quality progress.

In the military, during a crisis, the heads of divisions are given a minute each to report on their situation and what they are doing to improve it. With the sound of gunfire in the distance and everyone slightly dishevelled from recent combat, the meeting is incredibly focused. A few minutes and the job is done, everyone is informed, and progress can continue. Lives are at risk. There is no time to faff around.

If all of the team are on the same page and heading towards the *who, what, when* outcome, you will be able to make amazing progress in half the time.

This will shake things up, and they need a serious shake. So much time is being wasted in ineffective meetings. Very few *really* effective and progressive decisions are being made compared to the time and manpower being thrown at meetings. Cut them in half. Now. See how much you can achieve in this shorter, more focused time frame. Your corporate future will be much healthier because of it.

The zombies are going to hate it by the way. They will groan their discontent and tell you it can't be done. Be courageous. Take your machete to the typical laborious and nonsense meeting, and achieve your outcomes before the zombies have poured their coffee and ruminated over the biscuits.

A number of years ago, I had a small zombie-slaying application on my laptop. It would sit quietly in the corner of my desktop waiting to be loaded up with the number of meeting attendees and their average hourly wage. I would take an educated guess at the hourly rate, but the accuracy was not essential. At the start of a meeting, I would press the start button, and as the meeting progressed, it would display the total cost of the meeting so far. It's amazing how much money can be wasted before you've even had a pleasant 'catch-up' chat and eaten a few biscuits!

I had to remove the app after a while because it was causing too much distress to the professional timewasters in the organisation. Zombies, beware. The game must change.

Consider for a moment the outcomes from your recent meetings. Ponder the progress that has been made over the last few weeks. Could this be more? Could you and your team be more focused? The answer is yes, of course you can. Bring on brevity. Bring on better.

2 > 1+1

"Coming together is a beginning,
staying together is progress, and
working together is success."
— Henry Ford

Enabling each member of your meeting to excel at their role, to allow their talents to flourish with the end game in mind will revolutionise your team. To harness the power of many is a potent opportunity indeed.

If you are holding the get-together, you are in a superb position to enable the *brevity* revolution and remove the virus from your team.

Part of your role as organiser and guide during a meeting or group discussion will involve the facilitation of input from each participant. Active listening, accurate observation, and powerful use of body language will enable you to direct the audience and keep them on the brevity line. Keep them on message, apply clarity to the desired outcomes, and prevent ineffective deviation. You are in charge of surfing the communication waves and making sure none of your team slide into the perilous waters of the horde.

Old-School

As technology develops, the communication waters continue to rise with incredible speed. The flood of unproductive messaging will potentially devastate the majority of businesses, and if we're not careful, our relationships will be overcome too.

As mobile devices become more and more a part of who we are (I bet yours is within reach right now), the deluge will continue to adversely affect how well our communication lands and gets through.

Simply having your mobile device within view during a meeting will send a subliminal message to the rest of your group that they are not as important as your phone. If this thing *needs* me, I will respond. Even if you turn it so the face of your phone is hidden, the same rules apply — the zombie device rules.

I met with my financial advisor recently, and his phone stole the show. We met in my kitchen as I like to work from home and often have meetings over a cup of coffee. We sat and begun digging into the detail of some critical financial decisions. He placed his phone facedown on the table in front of him. Interesting.

It wasn't long (it never is) before it rang. He picked it up and had the decency to put it on silent. Down it went again, facedown. Now it's even worse. Someone has called, they have not been answered, and the phone is sitting there silent. The desire to pick it up and check who was calling is lingering in the air, and you can sense the pressure.

Crazy stuff really. How are we supposed to concentrate and focus on the task at hand if we voluntarily place an amazing distraction within arm's reach? Try to lose weight when an opened bag of crisps is sitting on your lap. Try to cut down on alcohol when your fridge is full to bursting with ice-cold, refreshing brews. It's not going to happen.

My advisor couldn't resist. At the first break in conversation, his hand darted to his phone to check who *needed* him. Disappointing.

Do not allow distraction to cloud your vision. Suggest that your meetings are mobile device free and see how that feels. I would expect resistance and more than a little grumbling. That will be the virus raising its head in concern. It's not as though we are asking our team to take any risks or put themselves in harm's way. We're simply removing the distractions. You will find that the improved focus, the added activity, and the dynamic results will be well worth the initial zombie groans.

We are always on. With such choice and variety for communicating, there is no surprise that taking a step back has an interesting impact.

Using the phone to make a voice call instead of an email, for example, will deliver a powerful impression that others are choosing not to make. Sounds daft, and it is, but a phone call has never been so powerful. Try it and see. Have voice to voice, human interactions, and make great things happen.

Pick up your phone and give someone a call. Right now. Scroll through your address book and select someone you are likely to email in the next day or so. Say hi and check in to see how they are. Let them know you are calling instead of pinging them an email as it has been a while since you've had a chat. How are the kids? What plans do they have for the weekend? How are they getting on with their business challenges? Where could you be of most help?

I suggested this to a group of university students at a recent talk, and you should have seen their faces. I find the younger generation extremely resistant to picking up the phone to make a voice call. It is not surprising; they have been brought up in a world that communicates in multiple ways, none of which require voice-to-voice contact. It is an unknown to many of that age group. How we encourage them to try this *alternative* option is quite a challenge.

One attractive reason to give a voice call a go is that it would definitely freak out the person on the other end of the call. How many of us are expecting the phone to ring and be greeted by a millennial? I am generalising here, but the trend is most definitely anti-voice. Even though there is superb value in hearing the tone of the conversation, and you can cover huge amounts of ground with ease, it is still the last option on many people's communication list. Voice is part of the cure. If we are concerned by the raging virus, we should all be making this a habit.

The go-to defence against picking up the phone tends to be based on a lack of trust. If I email you, I will have a record of what was said, and there can be no confusion as to who is at fault if things don't go according to plan. Just in case, to cover my back even more, I will cc everyone in too. Is this what it has come to? Trust is in such short supply that we daren't have a human conversation. Have the zombies taken over already?

Some interactions require evidence, are formal and legally binding, but not all of them. If we can't trust the people we are communicating with, what has happened to our business relationships? If it has to be recorded, then so be it. If not, we have a world of options.

The irony of our modern communication ocean is that it has never been easier to 'talk' to the world and share our ideas. We are only a few clicks away from global conversations, but global conversations are extremely noisy, and your voice will struggle to be heard.

There is no need to shout, but there is every need to get through.

Take your meetings by the balls and crank up the tempo, the passion, and the zeal. Chase the zombies out of the room and get stuff done! Stop adding to the ocean of noise that threatens to drown us all, and rely on email only when it is the best option, and even then, keep it focused. Have conversations that are rewarding as well as fun. Make progress and slay the horde as it attempts to drag you down into its meaningless noise.

SECTION 4

Becoming the Cure and Communicating with Your Audience

"...I don't just wish you rain, Beloved —
I wish you the beauty of storms..."
— John Geddes, *A Familiar Rain*

From time to time we will have the privilege to communicate with a group. These opportunities are growing in our digital world with the list of conferencing options growing week on week. At the time of writing, webinars,

Google Hangouts, and Facebook Live are in fashion, but by the time of reading these could easily have been surpassed by the rising stars of online mass communication. There is a question about attention and focus that many of these formats do not address, however. To dominate your audience's attention and draw them from their zombie slumbers in our connected age is a serious challenge; one which we must explore.

The corporate market still favours the good old presentation, although there should be nothing *old* about the presentations you make. The digital market has yet to match the power and connection that is possible during a live event, but it is getting closer. We don't need to attend an event to take away the key learning points any more. A digital version of the content is likely to be available somewhere and in various forms. We are getting to the point where we don't even want to attend an event because we are too busy trying to stay afloat in the ocean of zombie noise to find the time.

We may miss the excitement, the adventure, and the audience reaction if the real face-to-face presentation opportunity disappears, but will we be overly saddened if this is the case?

For many presentations I witness, sadly there would be little regret if we caught the content online.

Even a brief moment on stage should be immensely powerful. An unsurpassed opportunity to get inside the heads of your audience: to entertain, to educate, and stir them into action. No need for slides or notes, just impactful stories and communication insights — sounds zombie slayingtastic!

What an honour to have the audience's time and attention. These occasions are *gifts* which we should treat seriously; the impact of which should not be underestimated. Most of these *gifts* are poorly thought out, however, and belong in the pile of your Christmas box of biscuits or toiletry gift pack. Not inspiring or memorable at all. If you have an opportunity to share your magic with an audience, any audience, you must embrace it with everything you have and fully appreciate the significance that the occasion represents. Provide the best Christmas gift they've ever had!

This goes for the in-house company appearance, summarising what your team have been up to this quarter, and the 'lunch and learn' workshop you deliver to educate your teams. Your weekly report to management should be as important as the pitch to a new client to win a life-changing deal.

This is communication gold. Don't fritter it away as though it were small change.

It is becoming rare to have the undivided attention of an audience. Our world is evolving, and our communication technology is distracting us more now than at any point in history. It's rare to observe an audience at any kind of presentation that is not distracted by their mobile phones. Audience members may be tweeting your best bits or, more likely, catching up with their emails or scanning a variety of newsfeeds.

Far too many zombies are finding something more interesting to concentrate on while you're trying to share your magic.

Occasionally, even the presenter is distracted!

"OK, listen in everyone. I want to bring you up to speed and talk through the current state of play with the projects division. Hold on. Let me just check this text. Might be important. No, nothing urgent. OK, back to business. Eyes front, everyone. This shouldn't take too long. Erm, excuse me, at the back, can you leave your phone for a moment? And you. Come on, I'll be brief. Hold on. Sorry. This blooming phone won't leave me alone..."

If we are serious about affecting our audience's behaviour and having an impact that makes a difference, we have no other option but to step up. This may get uncomfortable for some of you. The virus will be raging, but battle through. We have a world to save.

Preparation

"You will never develop courage
if you don't stand in the middle of the
battle afraid and pick up the sword
anyways, to defend what is right. You
might feel like you are outnumbered,
but heroes always are."
— Shannon L. Adler

How long do you have? What type of presentation are you delivering? Are you appearing at an informal or formal event? What time are you in the limelight? What is the venue like? What technology do you need/will you have? How much preparation time do you need? How do you feel about your subject? The questions could go on.

All of these queries spring to mind before we even begin to consider our audience and our goals. Sadly, the answers to many of these questions seem to be rarely answered by the presenters I witness. We tend to leave quite a lot to chance, which is either very exciting or very foolish.

If in any doubt, ask the questions. Get a feel for the space and layout from the person asking you to speak. Explore in as much detail as is prudent the type of content and delivery they are expecting. If you can help it, don't walk in cold and unprepared. Take any opportunity you can to clarify what is to be delivered so you can plan and prepare accordingly.

Occasionally we have to deliver spontaneous presentations with no notice — the *could you just share your thoughts on this please* type of presentation. Sometimes you don't mind that when you're confident with your topic and happy to get stuck in. There are times, however, when you are put on the spot with no warning, and it comes as an unwelcome surprise. Rather unfair of the facilitator/host not to give you the heads-up, but we shouldn't shy away from the limelight if there's value in the opportunity. But how best can we prepare for the unexpected?

A glib solution to this problem is to always be prepared, always be ready. Easier said than done. A sensible answer is to be as ready as you can. Do your homework if there is even the slightest chance you will be called upon. Be as informed as possible, and you will ensure the experience for you and your audience is given the best chance of success.

"If you believe you can accomplish everything by "cramming" at the eleventh hour, by all means, don't lift a finger now. But you may think twice about beginning to build your ark once it has already started raining."
— Max Brooks, *The Zombie Survival Guide: Complete Protection from the Living Dead*

I remember preparing for a talk that ultimately took a very unexpected turn. I had been booked to speak to a university public speaking and debating society. I love these kinds of events. The audience, on the one hand, so hungry to learn, and on the other, so educated and ready to question. I had spoken with the client on more than one occasion before the event to explore exactly what would represent the best value for them and the type of audience we were dealing with. It was in a room I was familiar with, so there should have been no surprises. Well, life is full of surprises, as we know. Wouldn't it be dull if it weren't?

I arrived and made my way through the campus, my old student experiences sparking vivid memories. As I neared the lecture theatre, I spied signs that were directing me to another room. Interesting. I always aim to arrive early, my boarding school and military-style upbringing allows for nothing else, and I suggest you do the same whenever possible (arrive early, not attend boarding school). The *new* room where the talk was scheduled was laid out differently to what I was expecting. There was a huge projector ready for use, which was strange as I had no slides. To really ramp up the excitement, the audience was expecting a different topic than the one I had prepared!

Very interesting.

Sometimes all your preparation leads to very little, but usually it is still time well spent.

On this occasion, a chat with my client revealed what had happened. They were in a transitionary period between two group leaders. My client was the outgoing host, and the evening had been organised by the incoming chief. Oh.

First thing to do, smile and breathe. Not a massive problem. I know my craft and my subject, and this was not my first time thinking on my feet. Second thing to do was to turn off that giant projector.

Next step, and this is a real gem and will stand you in great stead going forward, take control.

When there is uncertainty, firstly listen, understand the situation as much as you can, and then take control of the solution, take ownership, and step into the breach. If you have listened well, you can plan a resolution that works best for all parties. Take the pressure off your host and allow yourself to be placed in the 'that guy is amazing' bracket.

I delivered my talk in the style of a Q & A which explored all the areas the audience were really interested in. I weaved in the content that both 'hosts' were looking for in my answers. I had a load of fun too, and so did the audience. A fabulous outcome for all involved.

Fortunately, I know my subject of 'communication' well, and I carry my metaphorical machete with me everywhere. The zombie horde shouldn't stand a chance.

Goals Worth Scoring

"If you want to live a happy life,
tie it to a goal, not to people or things."
— Albert Einstein

Your first consideration should be the goals you are looking to achieve through your interaction with your audience. Traditionally there will be two sets of goals: one set that you want to achieve for you, and another set you are looking to achieve on behalf of your audience. Zombie presenters simply lack any focus in this area. That's why they should be avoided if possible.

Without these goals firmly placed at the forefront of your mind, fully considered, and clearly defined, it would be impossible to know if your presentation has been a success.

If these goals are not in place, it begs the question why are you presenting at all? What are you playing at? The answer to that question is likely to be one of your goals, so that's a good start.

Be extremely clear about what a superb outcome looks like for you and for your audience. If you are looking to win new business, then how much, from who, and how will we know that this process is underway? Clarity down to pounds and pence, number of leads, and new clients on the books will have you focused in the right areas if new business is your goal.

If you are looking to inform and educate your audience, what markers will there be to show they have taken your content on board? What will change, what practices will be evident, and what outcomes will you be responsible for?

Most zombie presentations lack a clear goal. This is reflected in how many of these *performances* you have endured without being able to recall even a piece of the message. Think about the last three talks you attended. What can you remember? What are you doing differently now because of the information you received?

My guess is nothing! It's gone. We sit among so many audience moments, but only the rarest of the rare actually make a difference to our lives.

Typical goals I see presenters explore are to educate and entertain their audience, to look knowledgeable in front of their peers, to close a deal, to pitch for new business, to open doors to share wisdom, to instruct, protect, motivate, warn, deliver good/bad news, and to spread the word.

All these goals need some clarification though. We need to dig deeper to find what a successful outcome really looks like.

If we take one of the most common goals — to educate your audience — we can apply a host of questions to flesh this out and provide essential clarity.

To educate is to bring your audience new information in a way that sticks, that they can understand and use in the future. It is not good enough to deliver content and add to the noise. You have to get under their skin or nothing will change. Anyone in a teaching profession knows this to be true. Having the courage to do something about it is what we zombie slayers are here for.

I once suggested to a group of university students that if their lecturers were offering nothing more than dated and tired PowerPoint slides and were not sharing their genius through relevant stories and anecdotes, they should vote with their feet, get up, and leave. If the lecturer has not considered how to resonate with this audience, there will be more relevant, interesting, and entertaining options to experience the same content online (and I'm a huge fan of face-to-face communication, as you know). Until the students act, nothing will change. They are the customers, and their money should be wisely invested.

This did not go down well with the lecturers. No one ever said the zombies will appreciate our efforts to rid the world of their virus.

What practical applications can you use to demonstrate the *new* way of doing things? How can you highlight the value of your content? What happens if they all take the action you suggest? What does that look like? What success can we expect if we all change our behaviour? Will we be safer, more productive, richer, less stressed, or more effective?

What does 'educated' look and feel like for you and for your audience? When you know this, you can begin to plan how you can communicate in a way to make this happen.

And let's not forget about you. What does achieving an effective education for your audience do for you? What drives you to make this successful? If you are acting entirely altruistically and have nothing to gain apart from making the world a better place, then that is commendable. I wish you every success.

If, however, you would like to achieve something other than philanthropic kudos, then we need to consider how best to include your desires into your content, delivery, and impact.

Consider what a superb outcome would be, and align this with delivering massive value for your audience. Aim to achieve both, and you will know what a successful presentation looks and feels like. Then you can plan a zombie-free delivery.

Knowing Your Horde

"Nobody looks like what they really are
on the inside. You don't. I don't. People
are much more complicated than that.
It's true of everybody." — Neil Gaiman,
The Ocean at the End of the Lane

If you walked into a crowded presentation space and had to deliver your magic from behind a curtain and were never allowed to see your audience, how would you cope?

What a daft idea. It would never happen, and I'd like to think you would never allow it to happen.

Crazy as it seems, however, so many communicators don't consider their audience before, during, or after they share what should be some powerful content. It's as though they're presenting from behind that curtain, and that sure is mighty foolish.

How on earth are you supposed to create content that resonates with your audience, moves them to action, and has genuine impact if you don't know who they are?

When was the last time you truly considered your audience? How old are they, what is their current corporate position, what stresses are they under, how much time do they have, what does their social environment look like? Add to this their feelings on this particular day — have they sat through many presentations already, have they just had lunch, do they want to be there? Plenty to take on board before you set fingers to keyboard and begin to create your PowerPoint slides.

I suggest you make sure you know the answers to all these questions before you create your content. If needs be, ask an audience member or the meeting organiser to give you the lowdown.

While you're at it, ask them if they want your information delivered in PowerPoint form. I bet they don't! Imagine if you had to present and you weren't allowed to use traditional slide and bullet-point format. Don't feel as though slides and bullets are your default. Explore what will work for this particular audience. What will resonate? What would you crave if you were in the audience?

When I speak at an event and let the organisers know I won't be using the 'big screen', they're initially surprised. This surprise is soon replaced by relief and followed by a certain amount of intrigue. PowerPoint is effective for a few things, but it is so commonly the go-to option for all presentations that no audience are inspired when you plug your laptop into the screen and fire up your slides.

Next time you're asked to present, consider your alternatives. Could you make use of a writable surface or flip chart? Could you draw your thoughts rather than rely on slides? Could you use your audience as props? Can you play a game that illustrates your point? Can you explore your topic through amazing stories?

Do you really need the slides as a crutch? Zombies do. You have a choice. You have alternatives.

Audiences are just like you. We know this because we've all been part of an audience. Occasionally we've enjoyed it and been thrilled by the person on stage. Often, we haven't! Too often.

Stop and think what it is that you enjoy about an event. What makes an impact on you and changes your perception? How could you create an environment within which the world begins to look different? When was the last time, if ever, you left a presentation and the world had altered?

When I talk about the modern Armageddon on stage and introduce audiences to what the modern zombie looks like, there is no going back. Our eyes are opened, and we begin to see what has been obvious for some time. I share stories about the zombie virus and show pictures I have taken of the modern zombies at large. We all recognise the scenes, and they are petrifyingly close to home.

Taking your audience on a journey of discovery is what you should be aiming for. It is so, so rare that you are communicated to in a way that makes a difference. It's not necessarily about your content; it's about you. Yours and your audience's success hinges on how well you share your genius with them, and what they then do with your magic.

What Weddings Tell Me About My Audience

Audiences are just like us. We are rather selfish. We want stuff that relates to us, talks to us, delivers the things we need. If your audience can't answer the question, 'what's in it for me?', there's trouble ahead.

Remember the last time you were at a wedding (not your own) and had to endure an extended period of photography as the bride and groom were pictured with all guests in a variety of group styles and sizes? Not the most exciting part of the wedding for the guests as you wait your turn for a glimmer of the limelight.

A month or so later when you meet up with the bride and groom, you may be *treated* to a tour of the wedding album. As you flick through the pages and reminisce, if you are polite, you will complement the beautiful bride and handsome groom on a memorable day. But what you're really looking for is to see *you* in print and check out how you look. Of course you do. Oh, there you are, near the back, looking good. Hold on. Nope. You've got your eyes closed!

We want *our* stuff. Things that resonate. What does that look like to you? That is what you must deliver. If you don't, you will be one of many presenters who splurge content, vomit information, and deliver mostly zero for your audience.

Stop delivering the zombie food that does nothing but permeate the thinnest of layers. Don't allow your message to be quickly dusted away in the nearest breeze of something more interesting. Give your audience something new and shock the virus right out of the undead.

Zombies Are Only Hungry for Brains

"Soon silence will have passed into
legend. Man has turned his back
on silence. Day after day he invents
machines and devices that increase
noise and distract humanity from
the essence of life, contemplation,
meditation." — Jean Arp

What real audience's hunger for is truth.
When was the last time a presenter shared the truth? Showed you how they truly felt? Gave themselves over to you and provided immense value?

Oh my, it's rare. There is massive value in sharing reality rather than a version of information that is spun to fit a particular shape. Can you remember the last time a presenter was brutally honest? You will remember; it has impact. It is memorable and makes a difference.

You know when it hits because it gets through.

It gets through.

It gets through.

Think about that for a moment or two.

You have this power and can make this happen. You can deliver and get through. Be prepared to put the work in and understand what will work for your audience. This will feel uncomfortable. That's the virus kicking against your human antibodies, fighting for control. You are the one in control. You decide.

The presentation I mentioned earlier, when the CEO informed us all that the sales and marketing teams were heading out the door, could have easily been delivered as several PowerPoint slides filled with *management* speak. This was an option. The CEO asked us all what we would prefer: PowerPoint or to simply be informed as to what was going on. We wanted the truth, so opted for the human delivery. No doubt this helped to turn a difficult conversation into a more manageable discussion.

Most of the examples you have seen are, no doubt, laden with content. You won't remember the content, but there's plenty of it. Stuff to fill your brain. Facts, figures, charts, percentages, and statistics. Add to this overwhelming and tedious mix a few acronyms, references, and historical assumptions, and you will have nourished the horde.

The humans in your audience will take nothing away, and you will have wasted their time.

How many presentations from the last month can you actually recall? What messages, if any, can you remember, and how many of these have you acted upon?

The answer is, no doubt, rather sad. You are not alone. The virus continues to spread.

Opportunities

> "Never doubt that a small group of
> thoughtful, committed citizens can
> change the world. Indeed, it is the only
> thing that ever has." — Margaret Mead

Think back to your last presentation/talk/conversation and consider to what degree you impacted your audience. What percentage of your listeners actually took your message on board and made changes to their behaviour? How were their next steps guided by your words and your time on stage?

If you believe everyone in attendance was totally on board and were racing towards change, then you're probably one of the finest presenters on the planet. You are likely to have the most amazing content imaginable and a delivery style to boot. Or, possibly, you suffer from a large ego and even larger delusion issues.

These are the opportunities that life-changing movements are made of. The greatest speeches in history spring to mind. Addresses that managed to change the direction of a nation. They are exceptional in every way.

> "Be the change you wish to see in the world."
> — Mahatma Gandhi

If half your audience is affected by your talk, you're doing better than most. A standard presentation impacts less than a handful of the audience. Zombie alert!

This stuff is not easy. It takes courage. You wield your machete and deliver your best for the audience, even if only a proportion of them are ready to hear it. One of my recent presentations had an interesting degree of impact, but the amount of change accomplished was far from healthy.

I was experimenting with the subject matter of my talk and trying it out on a friendly audience. I was asking them to be courageous and to learn a new communication *dance* to replace their over-reliance on emails and their tendency to hide behind PowerPoint. It's a lot to ask a middle-aged, corporate audience, but my message was constructed for them and aimed at change. Moderate success doesn't sound too great, but for those that glimpsed a different future and took positive steps in a new direction, this was an excellent result. The next time I deliver this style of talk, the degree of transformation will be on the up and up.

Most change, certainly in the corporate arena, tends to take time. The ocean of zombie noise that surrounds us, however, is not waiting. The waters are rising and will submerge us all if we don't learn a new way. Even the strongest 'old-school' swimmer who relies on email and PowerPoint will grow tired (their audiences stopped listening some time ago), and they too will begin to drown as the zombie waves crush them against the rocks.

We are so used to information being delivered at us from the presenter's viewpoint using tired and uninspiring methods that we have stopped trying to absorb the detail and can't take their content to heart.

We are infected with the most modern virus. A virus that is born from repetition, tawdry techniques, and fatigued communication technology. Look out into the audience and observe the zombies that years of bullet points have created. The zombies cannot be slayed by these kinds of bullets — you need to bring out the *big guns* or begin swinging alternative weapons.

Try presenting with no technology other than a microphone. Use the power of story to illustrate, and ask questions to bring your audience into the action. You'll be blown away by the fresh air you bring to the room.

For far too long we have sat passively in the audience and been showered by the virus. Slide after slide, bullet after bullet we groan (very quietly, us British audiences rarely complain) as the infection takes hold and our brains turn to mush!

The Armageddon requires us to be the change our audience is crying out for.

On Stage

"Give your soul to touch their hearts."
— Dominique Champault

You have an opportunity to make a difference. To communicate with a group and make things better for them, their business, and for you. You choose how this goes. It is ultimately up to you, and you should shoulder this responsibility with daring and enthusiasm.

Let's say your presentation is a weekly catch-up with your team. Expectations are low; your audience just wants to get it over and done with. I imagine you don't have an appetite for it either and would rather just email the details across and get on with your day.

You've delivered this kind of presentation so many times you could do it in your sleep, not that the audience would notice as they are far from switched on most of the time. You just have to get through it and have put a standard 'deck' together to fill your time with sales data, graphs, and statistics. Roll on the coffee break!

If this rings a bell, then that is the bell to signal you to STOP!

No more. The virus charges through your veins — time to begin your cure.

If you cannot deliver any more value than dry pieces of content on pre-prepared slides, then don't bother. You are wasting everybody's time. Just ping an email summary across to your team and carry on hiding behind your PC. Take your pay cheque and enjoy your zombie weekend.

This type of communication is dead. You may not think so because we still see it everywhere, and the above description is probably a little too close to the truth for many of us.

Rooms are filled with zombies who have been fed this communication nonsense for far too long, and the virus has infected far too many organisations.

Time to begin slaying! Shake up your communication and stir the hornet's nest. Younger businesses, start-ups, and organisations populated by millennials are already all over this.

If this sounds scary, then you're welcome. Time to take back control and make an impact that lasts.

Let's take the 'weekly catch-up' style presentation and see what we can do with it...

1. What does our audience *really* want?
2. What is a superb outcome for us?
3. What does our audience enjoy — at work and beyond? What makes them buzz?
4. What do they dislike? What bores them and turns them off?

Do 1, 2, 3, and avoid 4. Simple. In theory.

Put yourself in their shoes. You've been there; we all have. Keep the content down to a minimum, and only deal in the areas that really matter. Address what you want to achieve. Know exactly what this looks like, or have a pretty good idea, and craft your presentation around that, as well as what your audience wants. Deliver it in half the time.

Don't forget that what the audience wants may be very different from what you think they need.

Shape everything around what your team enjoys, and generate the buzz that will make things happen. Also share why you believe this is important for them, for the company, and for you.

Superb work. Deliver it with a smile, with good humour, and in a relaxed, conversational way, and things will get better.

Imagine you were addressing colleagues in a coffee shop. You're relaxed, have a latte to hand, and the conversation is passing among you with ease. Why do your team catch-up sessions have to be so different? Do you really need the slides? Can you clear the room of distractions? Can you create an atmosphere of relaxed, albeit important, conversation?

Consider your presence. Stand (or sit) tall, breathe, take regular pauses, and observe the reaction of your audience.

They are *your* audience, after all. You should know how best to communicate with them and what makes them tick. Go for it and own the results that your magical communication will deliver.

If you are presenting to a large group and delivering some wide-reaching material from stage, then you will need to craft some additional magic into your delivery. If you understand your audience and care about them, this should be easier than it sounds.

Again, deliver 1, 2, 3, and avoid 4. Your delivery will be *bigger* depending upon the size of the stage. Your gestures will be grander, and your body language will become part of the show.

The content may be similar, but the size of venue usually dictates the style of delivery. Tailor your show to suit the environment, whether it be a large stage (audiences of hundreds), meeting room (audiences of tens), or workshop (audiences of handfuls).

Typically, on stage, you have forty-five minutes to an hour, in a meeting an hour plus (although I would like to think we can bring meeting times way down if we focus and apply the brevity revolution), and in workshops a number of hours. The material is created to enable more interaction the more time we have to share the magic.

Stage: 45 minutes — make every one of them count
Meetings: 60 minutes — focus on getting stuff done
Workshops: 3+ hours — transform your audience — enable positive change

The less time you have, the more focused, controlled, and potent your delivery. Often on stage, you have little time to build rapport and develop a relationship, but this is still a must for an outstanding delivery. You just have to 'get it on' from the moment you appear and begin to slay those zombies at every step.

Body Talk

For the bigger stages, your body language will naturally develop. If it doesn't, you should apply a little 'super grow' to your non-verbal communication. Turn on the heat and, like a mouth-watering pie crust, rise to the occasion.

Your body should be working hard to enhance your messages. Every point met by an appropriate gesture, each issue delivered with an accompanying sign, and every conclusion enriched by suitable gesticulation. Now I'm not suggesting you 'ham' things up to the point that the performance does not resemble *you*, but I am advising you crank it up a notch or two.

There are three main points I want to cover.

[holding three fingers up]

The first is going to be a piece of cake.

[open arm, palms up gesture]

The second is going to be the difficult one.

[concerned expression, solid eye contact, nodding to engage and spread agreement]

The third one I don't have the answers to, but I am sure you can assist.

[shoulder shrug, amused and slightly confused expression]

From the audience's perspective, the bold gestures will make perfect sense. How you use the stage, your powerful and purposeful movement, your hands, and how your body talks will add massive value to the audience.

The way you allow your hands to talk, your gestures, are at the mercy of your '*teenage spiders*'. Your hands are like unruly, disobedient, and disruptive adolescents if you choose not to focus on what they are up to. I've seen senior figures on stage playing with imaginary belts, scratching, fiddling, clicking, clapping, and allowing their hands to travel around causing havoc to their flow and creating a massive distraction for the audience. Your *spiders* need to be under your strict jurisdiction. Know where they are and what they are up to throughout your presentation. If they have nothing to do, then keep them in sight and ready for when you need their help next. It won't be long before they are needed again to add value to your words and enhance your show.

Be the master of all your non-verbal signals. Use your magic and allow your energy to positively enrich your audience's experience.

Magnify and propel your body language to the point that it is an enhanced version of your normal persona. Watch as the virus flees from your audience.

Work hard at delivering quality eye contact for each part of your audience. Spend a moment looking directly at a particular person or area of the crowd, and then move on and provide another 'gift' (more eye contact) for an alternative section of your audience. Show them you care and that you are sharing your truth with them. It builds rapport and trust and will amplify your presence.

You won't be surprised to hear that our zombie colleagues are extremely poor at anything involving eye contact.

How believable, how passionate you are, how much you care about your subject, and how much your audience take away, will be a direct reflection on how much you put into your performance. Zombies deliver content, humans enable magic to happen.

Risk vs Reward

"You cannot swim for new horizons
until you have courage to lose sight of
the shore." — William Faulkner

I find that too many presenters, or those sharing information with a reasonable-sized group, play it ultra-safe. They
stick to the same tired formulas and see anything outside of
the *norm* as far too risky. 'Power up my laptop' is the de fac-
to battle cry of the jaded corporate presenter. It is tiresome,
and very few people enjoy this method of communication
any more (if they ever enjoyed it).

My advice is to leave these zombies way behind you
when you shine in front of your audience. Separate yourself
from the 'old-school' whose idea of risk-taking is buying a
lottery ticket!

Risk aversion is understandable but creates an environment where nothing magical happens and nothing changes.
We are surrounded by communication that fails to make its
impact felt. Opportunities are missed, moments fall short,
and amazing ideas fade due to poor delivery.

Time to stand your ground, make a difference, and change the world!

I recently spoke at an entrepreneur's event with an audience
of young business owners and those preparing themselves
to leave school and join the corporate roller-coaster.

My host had invited me along as the surprise speaker with an open remit:

"Speak about anything you wish, Nick, but can you make sure you involve the audience and make it interactive?"

Of course, it will be a pleasure!

My talk was about risk, and it was designed to help the young audience understand that taking risks is part of being an entrepreneur. As long as we fail fast, don't give up, and learn from our mistakes, we will have an incredible business journey.

Most young audiences (and the not so young) are not prepared to take measured risks as their education is dominated by strict guidelines and examinations that explore simply the right vs the wrong answers.

Subjects are taught in such a narrow, examination-obsessed way throughout, and getting things wrong is considered a detrimental blow rather than a learning experience.

Entrepreneurs think differently. Risk is OK. Embrace it. Learn from it. Improve continually.

Exploring this topic from stage and in the spirit of taking risk, I decided to try something out that I had never done before. This could not be rehearsed and would be experienced live, in front of 200 people.

To add to the fun, two volunteers joined me on stage to take this risk with me. The quality of the young minds in the audience was reflected in the fact that plenty of people volunteered without knowing what the *risk* was going to be.

Once the three of us were on stage and introductions were complete, the risk experiment was explained.

We had previously distinguished between the *radiators* and *drains* in our lives. We agreed that those few people that are constantly supportive, positive about our actions, and ready to assist in our endeavours, whatever they may be (our radiators) should be thanked for their support. I suggested we should acknowledge these people and tell them how much they mean to us and how grateful we are — over the phone, live on stage.

A series of phone calls live from stage... Rather risky and possibly a load of fun too.

I kicked things off and phoned my mum. She had no idea I was at the event, and she was not expecting my call. I had no idea how it would go, or even if she would pick up, but that was OK. This was *risk*, and that was the whole point, after all.

Out came the phone (on speaker setting) and a handheld microphone so my audience could hear everything. I dialled the number.

The audience were on the edge of their seats — waiting, anticipating, smiles on their faces. When was the last time you were in an audience and were on the edge of your seat?

My mum answered.

We said hello to each other, and I let her know we were live on stage, and I was sharing our conversation with 200 others. I expressed how grateful I was for her support, how much I appreciated everything she had done for me and my kids, and how much I loved her. It was an emotional sharing of my truth. My mum was blown away by it, and so was the audience. There were tears.

It was risky, impactful, and memorable.

My volunteers followed suit, and similarly emotive and fun exchanges took place. The audience was totally transported through each of these phone calls, and we managed to stir their emotions and deliver a message few will forget in a hurry.

Risky? Oh yes. Worth it? Most definitely.

Information delivered in a way that moves, that impacts, creates change, and makes things better.

How does my audience consider the subject of *risk* going forward? Very differently than they did before my twenty minutes of crazy stuff, that's for sure. No room for zombies here.

If the subject of your presentation allows it, and you are not taking risks on stage, you are missing an opportunity and letting your audience down. *You* are communicating with your audience for a reason: your knowledge, your experience, your position in the company, or your recognised ability to engage with the crowd, so embrace this opportunity to the full and deliver *magic*.

Have a quick think about your last or your next presentation and check it for *risk* factor. Did you or are you taking any measurable risk? If not, why not? What are you afraid of?

You're probably afraid of the following:

- Looking a fool
- Being misunderstood
- Things going wrong
- Upsetting some audience members
- Making a career-defining mistake

This is what risk looks and feels like though. Without these fears, the risk wouldn't be risk at all; it would be vanilla, the norm, what we see again and again, zombie, zombie, zombie.

It used to be much easier to communicate in a way that gets through. We weren't all drowning in the noise of the zombie horde. We stood a reasonable chance of being heard, and some of our messaging would resonate with our audience. These days it takes great courage to get through because we are increasingly required to do things differently, and to start with that is a scary place to be.

Now is the time to dare to be human. There are too many zombies out there. We can't afford to lose you too.

Don't Expect to Get it Right All the Time

"D'oh!" — Homer Simpson

In my very early days as a speaker and trainer, I had an opportunity to work with a large team to enrich their communication techniques. It was a really healthy opportunity for me to share my craft. The client was a big deal, and their credentials would prove a superb testimonial — it had to go well.

I travelled the lengthy distance to the client's office, going over my content and fine-tuning my approach and delivery.

Part of my plan was to illustrate that a poor opening when communicating is difficult to recover from and usually an indicator as to how the rest of the performance is going to go. To demonstrate this, I referenced a school musical recital. The young performers take to the stage with their recorders, ready to delight their adoring parents with a brief and basic tune. From the very first note, you know what you are in for. If it begins well and the first note is hit, you can relax. It will be fine and will soon be over. If it begins poorly, you are in for a rough ride. As the first note squeaks and squeezes its way out of the lifeless piece of plastic, all you can do is fix a false smile on your face to hide the grimace and hold on. It will be over, eventually.

To illustrate this even more, I had brought my guitar along. At the appropriate moment, it was time to bring out my musical prop and bring on the risk. The plan was to ready my audience and build a little anticipation, and then play the start of a musical piece *badly*. I would then ask them how it made them feel.

The response I was looking for was 'uncomfortable' and not looking forward to the rest of the music. Just like a poor start to a presentation, it makes you fear what is to come — dah da. Point made, illustrated, and demonstrated — what a genius.

I thought it had gone well until I spoke with my host after the event. He was complimentary and thought his team took plenty away from the session, but he didn't get the guitar piece. He thought I had simply messed it up due to nerves and felt rather sorry for me!

What! How could he not have seen how well it had illustrated the point? I wonder how many others in the audience had shared his experience? Bugger.

That was years ago, but I still remember that my risky demonstration did not land as I'd thought, not with the entire audience anyway. Perhaps I should have blown them away with a masterful demonstration of guitar prowess after the 'bad' start to illustrate the difference, but I didn't.

Do I regret taking the risk? Nope. The memory makes me smile. I was brave, it was different, perhaps some of the audience still remember it for the right reasons. It was worth it. I am not afraid of doing things differently. If I am going to fail at something, I am willing to fail fast, learn, and carry on, improving all the time. Our journey is not one to shuffle through; we must live it! We are surrounded by the *undead* who are shuffling their way through opportunities to learn and to evolve but are too fearful to take anything from them.

I encourage you to take a few risks so you can look back at your journey with a proud smile and know you have made a difference. If we don't have adventures along the way, we won't have any stories to tell our grandchildren.

Too many of us are living our lives through the adventures of others, following their exploits online without daring to embrace our own.

Instant Audit

"I know it is wet and the sun is
not sunny. But we can have lots of
good fun that is funny!"
— Dr. Seuss, *The Cat in the Hat*

A quick check — how much fun are you having? Out of 20 this time. What is your score? Right now?

I'd like to think you are in the region of 15 and above as you are reading my book, or at least a 12, surely? Anything less, and you probably didn't make it this far through the book.

This is a healthy and somewhat scary exercise to run at multiple times throughout your day. It's possibly the most useful well-being exercise you can use, and it only takes a moment. Let's call it your *instant audit*.

You get up and have a relaxed breakfast with those you love, walk to work, and greet your colleagues with a smile — how much fun are you having?

You drag yourself out of bed, skip breakfast, rush out of the house, and sit in traffic for two hours and arrive late for work — how much fun are you having?

You're in a meeting and your team are summing up their monthly sales — how much fun are you having?

You're presenting your latest proposal to the board — how much fun are you having?

You're down the pub sharing stories with your friends — how much fun are you having?

You're relaxing over a latte with your best friend, listening to their relationship antics — how much fun are you having?

I'm writing this part of the book in Normandy on holiday. I've been for a run by the ocean, and the wind was buffeting but life-affirmingly fresh. I've breakfasted on French cuisine and have a day of adventure ahead. I am currently 19 out of 20 on the 'fun-o-meter', and it feels good.

My concern is that I meet too many people that struggle to make it to 10 out of 20, and they only manage this on rare occasions. It *looks* like they are struggling to have fun too. Is that any way to live?

Before you accuse me of simplifying life, I know things can be tough. I've had my fair share of struggles, challenges, and hurdles (opportunities) and will continue to do so. But ask yourself if you are happy with your current score. If you are, then that is superb. If not, then you have some choices to make.

Life is about choices — you make them all the time, and if you are not as happy as you would like to be, then make some better choices. Sound too easy? Give it a try.

When you are communicating, assess your score. Imagine the score of your audience too. If you have crafted your messages for them, I would like to think their scores are looking healthy.

The numbers don't really matter; it's how you feel about your current number that really counts.

If you want it to be higher, take action. You only get one go at this life, so choose to live it with a smile on your face.

Make a decision right now to increase your *audit* number. What could that look like? What would it entail?

I have just stopped writing and taken the slightly odd opportunity to play some 'kitchen ping-pong' with my son. It was a little crazy but made us both smile, and we escaped from the world for a moment or two. *Audit* number up one notch.

Whatever is going on in your world, you can choose to respond in a way that serves you and your audience. Even the toughest stuff provides room for choice.

Recently I had the pleasure of sharing the stage with John Nichol. John was an RAF navigator and on the first British plane to be shot down during the Iraq conflict. John tells an extremely compelling account of how his Tornado aircraft was bombarded by anti-aircraft fire, and how he and his pilot were forced to eject seconds before their plane exploded into the Iraqi desert. Both airmen were captured, held, and tortured for seven weeks before eventual release.

An extreme example of the 'tough stuff' without a doubt, but still John had a choice as to how he responded to his ordeal. One of the most striking moments of his entire presentation was when he explored the consequences of everything that went on during that fateful mission and the seven weeks that followed. Given the chance to turn the clock back, John would not change the experience. He chooses to make positivity his mantra, and he's crafted an amazing career on the back of positive and healthy choices.

He continues to respond in a way that serves him and his audiences. It was awesome to be able to share a piece of the magic.

If you can increase your audit number by a tiny margin, do it now. The zombies don't know how, but we have the power of choice on our side.

Virus Symptoms

"Failure is the condiment that gives
success its flavour." — Truman Capote

So much of our communication is hindered by fear. We
stick with the norm, the *safe*, or what we consider to be
safe, because we don't want to get it wrong. Our fears will
hold us back and prevent us from sharing our magic with
the world.

For me, fears are as real as they are for you. I choose to
ignore them most of the time and dive into the new orbit.
Fear is often based on our assumptions about a particular
situation or set of circumstances. We tend to dwell on the
negative rather than assuming the positive.

*What if I try something new in front of my team,
and it doesn't go well? What will they think of me? I'd
better not risk it.*

*What if I try something new in front of my team, and
it goes great? What will they think of me? I'd better
risk it.*

Such a similar process with the smallest of changes can
make all the difference.

*What if it doesn't go well, but they think I am amaz-
ing for trying?*

So often the *what if* creeps into a scenario to guide us to a *safer* outcome. This is a massive shame because the *what if* can so easily be utilised to propel us into an amazing outcome if we decide to approach it from an adventure standpoint rather than a fearful one.

The zombie's favourite saying is '*I would but…*'. Don't let this slip into your vocabulary.

I would begin jogging, but I don't have the time.

I would give up smoking, but not while this project is in full swing.

I would ask her out on a date, but I'm petrified of looking a fool.

I would cut down on my drinking, but I'll wait until after BBQ season.

I would take more risks on stage, but I don't want to look inexperienced.

We have to get off our *buts* if we want to fight the virus and prevent the zombies from taking over our world.

Our fears prevent us from standing out and volunteering to present to our team. Our fears prevent us from putting our hand up and offering our opinion. Our fears prevent us from asking the girl of our dreams for a coffee date. Our fears prevent us from taking a chance, from leaping into the unknown, from embracing the adventure and having fun.

Fear will hold you back, again and again and again. It is stopping you from being the true you and sharing your truth with the world. The zombies are coming. They can smell your fears!

We are assuming the negative, and it is making us unhappy, so stop it! From here on in, join me by assuming the positive, embracing the fear, the adrenaline, the heart-pumping awesomeness that shows you are alive and giving your all.

The reality is that once you embrace the unknown, the fear recedes, if not disappears completely.

Consider the first time you went on a particular roller-coaster. You approach it and it looks huge, even from a distance. As you assess the loops and the corkscrew madness, your heart lets you know this is a bad idea. You are nervous and for good reason. The ride is designed to push that uneasiness to its limit.

If you are brave enough to join the queue of excited thrill-seekers, your fears multiply. You can hear the screams of the riders and the thundering roar of the coaster cars. It's the sound of torture, not one of fun. If there was an option to exit without walking past all those in the queue behind you, it would be a serious possibility.

You're strapped in and holding on as though your life depends on it, and the ride begins to climb. Slowly creeping upwards and upwards. Your heart is ready to bounce right out of your chest. And then the fun really begins.

You survive. You scream, you laugh, you may even shed a tear, but you survive.

Once you are off and safely on the ground, you can look at the *beast* you have ridden with new eyes. You may jump straight back in the queue for another go, or you may need to sit down and rest your swaying head, but the ride is no longer the fear-inducing monster it was at first sight.

You have experienced it, and whether you enjoyed it or not, you know what it has in store. You have the knowledge that allows you to assess if you want to have another go or not. Your choice is no longer influenced by fear.

Fear shrinks once you have had a go. The more you do something, the smaller the fear. Have a go and get the first attempt out of the way, then you can decide if you want to have another go.

Overcoming Nerves

Practise, rehearsal, and a dry run will reduce your nerves, guaranteed. Rehearse again and again until the nerves are minimal. The first time you do something new is usually scary, or exciting depending on how you want to look at it, but the second is normally much less of a task, and the third even less of a challenge.

For some, this is reassuring as it will make your performance less hindered by nerves. For others, multiple repetitions will make things stale and be an indication that new challenges are required.

Do it and do it again. This will help. The first time is the hardest, but do it anyway — amazing things await. Don't forget to celebrate once you have made it through that first time.

You could even use your first go at everything as a practice run. Volunteer, take the plunge. Then do it again for *real*.

Even More Opportunities

There are opportunities everywhere for you to communicate with strangers, with your tribe, and with larger groups. If you seek them out, they are there.

If you want to find them, you will find them. You can then work your magic into your message and share your truth with the world.

The adventures await. My younger self could not see them, could see nothing more than a world filled with dread and concern for what was around the next corner. My younger self could not embrace the unknown and take measured risks to add flavour to the journey. My younger self needed to change, to grow, and to explore. Fortunately, he did, and I am relishing opportunities that have materialised since.

There are conversations to be had with people you don't yet know. There are moments of magic to share with your team. There are occasions when you can dominate your stage and share views, experiences, and knowledge with an audience hungry for direction.

You've just got to reach out and take a chance.

Zombie Slayer

"The exhilarating ripple of her voice
was a wild tonic in the rain."
— F. Scott Fitzgerald, *The Great Gatsby*

What you must offer these strangers, your team, and the wider audience is *your voice*. My younger self did not know his own voice. He didn't share his thoughts, opinions, or beliefs. All his magic was hidden, protected by a lack of nerve. In our zombie-ravaged world, we can't afford to hide or cower away from the virus.

Your Voice

Your voice needs to be set free. There are a host of people who can and will benefit if you begin to share the real you and communicate with the courage, passion, and hunger they deserve.

Do you deliver the corporate message in keeping with all previous deliveries that have come before? Or do you provide your unique take on the content, using your stories in a style that is all yours?

Sadly, most of what I see and hear is the former, and it does nothing to shift the virus. Too many audiences are filled with jaded zombies addressed by presenters who do nothing but feed the infection with incessant noise.

You must do better than that. We have to hear from you. From the heart, the real you, honest, authentic, emotional you. Give yourself, and you will feel a shift in the room. The zombies will feel uncomfortable, the hold of the modern disease will begin to loosen, and you will be able to carve a new future for you and all those who are lucky enough to share your presence.

Your voice has incredible value, and you should not allow it to remain hidden and unheard. There are too many zombies that need to hear what you have to offer. The world needs you.

The virus stops here. You are the cure.

Once you step into your new orbit, you will begin to formulate *your voice*. The more you step outside the norm, the more you will have to share.

Consider your personal brand. What do you stand for? What do you represent?

My brand stems from my authenticity — I'm quirky, fun, optimistic, and solid, and my approach to communication is reflected in these values.

The strength of your brand will be perceptible in what your audience are left with once you have left the room. Will you be talked about? Will your message be understood? Will your audience heed your advice and take steps in a new direction? Will the communication ocean feel your waves of progress, or will your content drown in the swirling eddies of noise?

Storytelling

One of the most potent and, strangely, easy ways to unleash your voice and share amazing ideas with your audience is through the power of storytelling.

Stories have been used throughout the centuries, enabling information to be absorbed, understood, and utilised in an easy to digest and readily available way. You already tell stories daily, so the jump to communicating powerfully through storytelling is a simple one.

Take any story — audiences love good news stories by the way — explore what lesson it illustrates, and consider how the retelling of this tale can add value while being simple to absorb.

I have hundreds of examples, and so do you. Even if you don't think you do.

Consider your journey to work. How did it go, what did you learn, what point does it illustrate? What about that meeting you were late for or the time you were assisted by a stranger? Remember when your kids got you into trouble and what you all learnt from the experience? The time when you did some work on your home and you certainly bit off more than you could chew. Or the time you were amazed by someone's tenacity, courage, ignorance, cheek, calm etc. Think, and they will come.

With a little thought, you can amass a host of stories that illustrate every aspect of your truth, to paint a picture for your audience and enable others to see exactly what you are trying to say.

It makes sense to collate your stories in a notebook as and when they occur. This way you can pick and choose the story that fits your message best. If you are diligent and write at least one down a day, you will never be short of a suitable anecdote.

The reason stories are so powerful is that they make better use of your brain than the simple delivering of content ever does. If you digest typical content, a single part of your brain is responsible for interpreting and processing the information received. Not a great deal happens. Stuff goes in, it may or it may not be recalled.

When you are told a story, every sense that is activated lights a separate firework of activity in your brain. So much more of your grey matter is involved in the process. This is one of the reasons that well-told stories are so easy to remember and retell.

Sadly, I come across far too many zombies who are fearful of sharing their stories. They tend to wear a cloak of formality. I would tell stories, but that's not how we do things around here. It isn't considered professional. I don't have time for anything but the facts.

When was the last time you heard a story and it stopped you in your tracks? I bet it was more recent than that non-existent time when a PowerPoint slide made you sit up and take notice.

Be Part of the Story

How about a bit of interactivity? Bring those zombies back from the dead by including them in the action! If you can enhance how the audience receives your messages by involving them in your story, you will be reaching new heights in the hearts and minds of those you wish to inspire.

Ask some questions, get people on their feet, raising a hand, choosing an option, or sharing an opinion. Try referring to individuals in the audience, not necessarily by name, and don't feel as though you need to single them out, but embrace their part in the journey and celebrate their participation.

"Wow, this is not like most of the presentations I go to. It's as though I'm being spoken with rather than to — interesting."

The need to shake things up and provide an alternative perspective has never been stronger. Audiences have never been hungrier for your magic than they are right now.

Don't be like most presenters and disappoint your horde. Open their eyes and chase the virus clean out of their veins.

What Next?

If you have worked hard, considered your audience, and set healthy goals for your group's communication, you will have a chance to make a *real* difference. You should not shy away from this opportunity. Prepare for it with an effective call to action.

Your call to action should be part and parcel of your delivery, not an add-on that you squeeze in at the end. This is an integral part of the journey that you have guided your audience along. It is a key part of your communication, and your goals should not be complete unless your message is absorbed and acted on.

How many times have you sat in a room and been talked at? Information has been shared by the guide at the front of the room, and you had no idea what you were supposed to do next (if anything) with the *wisdom* that you painfully and patiently sat through.

Most audiences shuffle away from a presentation more infected by the virus than when they sat down. Their thoughts are dominated by coffee, escape, and brains.

It's like sitting through a film that has lost the final scene — you end up wondering 'what was that all about?'

Imagine watching *Titanic*. The ship hits the iceberg, and all hell breaks loose. The waters rise, and the passengers and crew are panic-stricken. The ship begins to go down, and the heart-stopping cold of the invading water consumes the beauty of the once magnificent vessel. The music rises with the icy waters, and the credits roll! What? Hold on. Where is the rest of the film?

We may not like the ending, we may want an alternative outcome, but we most definitely deserve the closure that the end of the film delivers.

Your presentation without a call to action is a bit like that. You have set the scene, shared your story, delivered your truth, but we don't know what happened to Rose or Jack!

A bit mean of you really to let your audience down like that. They are not likely to queue up for your next performance.

Even if your only goal is to educate your audience, you still need them to do something with their new knowledge, to use it, to remember it, to share it etc. Whatever it is, your audience needs telling and motivating to take the appropriate action.

As a basic guide, weigh up your goals — those key points you thought through in detail before you constructed your communication piece. Have these been realised? Does your audience have clear instruction as to how they can make these goals a reality? Have you provided enough clarity around what these look like and the steps to making them happen?

If your goal was to secure five new clients, have you made it easy for the audience to take the steps required to make this a reality? If the first part of your acquisition process is a face-to-face meeting to explore opportunities, then make sure you give the audience explicit instructions as to how they book and take part in one of these meetings. Make it clear, make it simple, and motivate them to take appropriate action.

Not until you are certain you have given yourself and your audience the best opportunity for success can you be secure in the knowledge that the zombies are held at bay. There is still slaying to do, but you are wielding your machete like a pro.

Adventures in Zombieland

"Courage starts with showing up
and letting ourselves be seen."
— Brené Brown, *Daring Greatly*

However you communicate, you need to take ownership. The risk and rewards you share with the audience, but the most exciting choices are yours to make.

Getting through is not easy, but it is essential. There may be one or two barriers to overcome.

I thought I would test my theory of the power of getting through a little while ago, and what better place to put it to the test than the most hostile communication environment I know. London's tube service.

No one talks on London's underground system; we're all too squeezed in and uncomfortably invading each other's space. The overall perception is that the tube is not a place to converse.

In other words, an ideal place to test what getting through looks and feels like.

On this particular day, I had been to a trade show and had picked up a squidgy stress ball. The carriage was not quite full, but the air was heated by the presence of too many bodies, and we were rocked from side to side as the train squealed its way along the tracks. No one stirred, no one spoke, not even a passing glance was made at the guy flexing the stress ball — until he opened his mouth.

"Why don't we have a game of catch?"

Oh, look out. There's a crazy guy on board. Not only is he talking, but he's suggesting we play a game!

Quick, all eyes on the floor. No one wants to make eye contact with the crazy dude. The other passengers were shrinking into themselves in the vain attempt of avoiding the limelight.

I may be a little (or a lot) quirky, but I am not daft. I knew my fellow 'players' would need some reassurance and some encouragement. We were on the Central Line and fast approaching the busy Oxford Circus station. I mentioned this to my carriage of unwilling participants and suggested that at the next stop more people would get on, and then we could have a really exciting game of catch. They were not convinced.

Oxford Circus came and went, and more people did indeed get on. I noticed that nobody got off. No one took the opportunity to escape and change carriages. In my mind, this meant game on!

As the train pulled out of the station, the game began.

What would you do if you were on the tube and a game of catch erupted? What choice would you have?

My first throw was to a young lad, who it transpires was visiting London from Germany. He caught the ball and threw it back. Excellent. I then threw it to another passenger who similarly caught it and threw it back. And then, something tiny but magical happened. I threw the ball to another traveller, and they threw it to somebody else.

The game was no longer about this crazy dude and his squidgy stress ball. The game had evolved and now belonged to us all.

From here the play really picked up pace. The ball was flying from one person to the next in completely random fashion. A number of times it progressed to one of the central parts of the carriage, where people were standing by the doors, and it made its way back. It then worked its way from our part of the train, past the people standing, through the very centre of the carriage, and into the third section of the playing area (as far as it could go), and for some reason, it didn't come back.

At this point, the young German lad was peering down the length of the tube, shaking his head. In a somewhat distressed tone, he told me the ball wasn't coming back.

My response was to let him know that it didn't matter but to have a look around. We were now surrounded by people laughing, talking, interacting like they didn't have a care in the world — on the tube.

We had broken down all of the communication barriers and turned a carriage full of zombies into a group of smiling and talking animated humans with a game of catch.

Risky? Perhaps. Courageous? Probably. But what a difference it made to the rest of the journey. I like to think that if you were on the tube that day, you will remember the simple game of catch and how it made you feel. One thing is certain, we got through and made a massive impact.

Share the risk and the reward, but be brave enough to make some interesting choices.

Props

I have used squidgy stress balls on a number of occasions since that day to illustrate a host of different points in my talks and workshops. It is a very useful prop, and my audiences love it too.

Consider your next talk, presentation, or meeting and think creatively as to what props you could use to make people think differently and transform how they see the issues at hand.

In my *Invisible PowerPoint* show, I juggle with lemons to prove a point about the use of visuals. I have also seen creative use of eggs, apples, tennis balls, sports equipment, kitchen utensils, a globe, a clock, and even a fully-fledged Hollywood film trailer. Bill Gates famously released a number of mosquitos in his hard-hitting TED Talk to highlight the plight of those struggling with the fight against malaria. If you were in any of these audiences, I imagine you remember the props used and the impact they had.

If they are used well and have a fitting and powerful purpose, they will transform your delivery and your audience — most definitely worth experimenting and taking a few risks with.

The time is ripe for your communication experiments. Lift the heads of the zombie horde by interacting in a fresh and novel way. You and they will be amazed at what can be achieved.

Don't Mention the E-Word

You've only gone and done it, Nick. You mentioned the E-word. Actually, I've mentioned it in excess of twenty times, and that's OK.

It's OK to show, share, and use your emotion. This has been one of the hardest tasks for me as I have grown into a modern zombie slayer. I used to find it extremely uncomfortable and didn't think there was a place for it in corporate communication. How wrong I was.

I'm not suggesting we shriek, wail, and cry our way through meetings, although I can imagine you've been to one or two that have stirred these emotions in you. I'm not suggesting we shout and bellow at our audience or whimper on a stranger's shoulder. I truly believe we must give honesty, authenticity, and the courage to stand out from the crowd.

This can only truly be achieved if we invest emotionally in our communication. Dig deep and feel that what we say, the messages we send, and the content we deliver, is our truth and is a part of who we are.

It is not a contradiction to be in control of your emotions and still communicate with feeling and share your passion. If your audience doesn't feel it, they are unlikely to change. If you do not share your hunger, don't expect your colleagues to join the feast.

Zombies traditionally hunger for brains. The modern zombie is similarly sated by data and information. Our connected world provides infinite knowledge with ease. The zombies are satisfied only temporarily before they renew their echoing moans and hunger for more. More noise, more diversion, more nonsense.

Most of your audience is twitching to get their hands back on their digital distractions, to lose themselves in the virus. Our job is not to feed this disease, but to cure it, and that will take emotional courage and a range of alternative *weapons*.

If you want to make a real difference, allow your dissatisfaction to shine and glimmer off your machete as you carve a difference into the world.

Practise

I'm not suggesting you jump out of the plane without practising how it feels to fly, but I am suggesting you spread your wings and take to the air. You can begin small: a conversation with a stranger on the train, using a story or anecdote in your next meeting, taking a potential prop onto stage — just its presence will make your audience think.

You have to begin. The world needs you soaring above the heads of the horde, so you need to find your wings and start.

The more you step into a new orbit, the less the virus will grip you and hold you back.

Have a go. Do something unexpected, alternative, and a tiny bit risky. See how it feels, and see how your audience reacts. Have immense courage to do it again. Be brave and brandish your machete with the strength of the professional slayer you are destined to be.

There Are No Shortcuts

"You take people, you put them on a
journey, you give them peril,
you find out who they really are."
— Joss Whedon

Imagine you are travelling through a busy city and are presented by two choices. One route is lined with escalators: crowded, predictable, moving at a fixed pace. The other route is lined with steps: challenging but empty. Which would you choose?

Most will opt for the escalators, which is understandable. They are easier, often quicker, and reasonably effortless. I suggest you take the stairs. Unless you are laden with shopping or escorting the elderly, always take the stairs.

The modern zombie opts for the easy and the convenient. The virus persuades us to allow the technology to do all the work. Our technology does not register sentiment, does not look to empathise or resonate with our audience. The digital solution may be simple, swift, and cheap, but it pays a costly price. Zombie communication does not get through.

There are no shortcuts in the zombie Armageddon. There is courage, strength, and better ways to communicate, but don't expect these to be the easy option. The escalators are filled with the virus-ridden undead looking for a quick fix, a simple and effortless route. Their journey leads nowhere, however. Nothing changes, and there is no getting through.

The stairs require effort, spirit, and the energy to make a difference. You can walk, run, even dance up the stairs. Your direction and progress are yours. You are not on the conveyor belt. You are in control of your own destiny.

Don't look for the shortcut. Be a better way.

There is no need to judge the zombie; they cannot see life through the lens of virus-free communication at present. You will experience them everywhere. They haunt your office, fill your auditoriums, plague you with emails, groan at you in traffic, and swarm to your social media feeds.

They spread their virus with every shuffling step. Stay strong.

We can wake them from their undead slumbers and be the antibiotic for the virus that charges through their veins. But it will take real grit.

We are the antidote to a world that is forgetting how to interact in a human way. The way ahead is not yet blocked, but it is crowded with communication noise, and it is beginning to overwhelm. As technology improves and alternatives to human communication abound, the fight will intensify. This is our battleground. You are not alone.

We are the answer.

Fight the virus and free the world.

I am extremely keen to hear from you and look forward to sharing stories of zombie slaying at work, at home, and beyond. Please feel free to contact me by one of the means below and share your journey. Us survivors should stick together.

Nick's mobile human-conversation device: 07800 662450

Nick's a little-less-human email: nick@feetontheground.co.uk

No zombies, living or undead, were harmed
in the writing of this book.

The horde should be worried though
'cause we're coming to get you!